DATE DUE

DEMCO 38-297

"WE'LL STAND BY THE UNION"

MAKERS OF AMERICA

"WE'LL STAND BY THE UNION"
Robert Gould Shaw
and the
Black 54th Massachusetts Regiment

PETER BURCHARD

Facts On File

"We'll Stand By the Union": Robert Gould Shaw and the Black 54th Massachusetts Regiment

Copyright © 1993 by Peter Burchard

Facts On File, Inc.
460 Park Avenue South
New York NY 10016

Library of Congress Cataloging-in-Publication Data
Burchard, Peter.
    "We'll Stand by the Union": Robert Gould Shaw and the Black 54th
Massachusetts Regiment/Peter Burchard.
        p. cm.—(Makers of America)
    Includes bibliographical references and index.
    ISBN 0-8160-2609-2
    1. Shaw, Robert Gould, 1837–1863. 2. United States. Army.
Massachusetts Infantry Regiment, 54th (1863–1865) 3. Massachusetts—
History—Civil War, 1861–1865—Regimental histories.
4. Massachusetts—History—Civil War, 1861–1865—Participation, Afro-
American. 5. United States—History—Civil War, 1861–1865—
Regimental histories. 6. United States—History—Civil War,
1861–1865—Participation, Afro-American. 7. Soldiers—
Massachusetts—Biography. 8. Afro-Americans—History—To 1863.
9. Afro-Americans—History—1863–1877. I. Title. II. Series:
Makers of America (Facts on File, Inc.)
E513.5 54th.B83 1993
973.7'415'092—dc20
    [B]   148402   92-37132
A British CIP catalogue record for this book is available from the British
Library.

Text design by Debbie Glasserman
Jacket design by Duane Stapp
Composition by Grace M. Ferrara/Facts On File, Inc.
Manufactured by R.R. Donnelley & Sons, Inc.
Printed in the United States of America

10 9 8 7 6 5 4 3 2 1

This book is printed on acid-free paper.

For Linda

Right in the van,
On the red rampart's slippery swell,
With heart that beat a charge, he fell
Foeward, as fits a man;
But the high soul burns on to light men's feet
Where death for noble ends makes dying sweet.

JAMES RUSSELL LOWELL, 1863
Memoriae Positum R.G. Shaw

CONTENTS

ACKNOWLEDGMENTS

In writing this biography, I made constant use of the Williams College Sawyer Library. Thanks partly to my friend and counselor Fredrick Rudolph, who instituted a black studies program at the college in 1965, the Sawyer has become an important source of material on black history—the slave trade, slavery in America, the antislavery movement and the Civil War. At the Sawyer, Librarian Phyllis Cutler and Assistant Librarian Jim Cubit have, under their direction, patient and delightful men and women. Most helpful to me was the reference team—Lee Dalzell, Peter Giordano, Walter Komorowski, Helena Warburg and Karen Worley. Thanks to Circulation Supervisor Jo-Ann Irace and her staff.

Thanks to the staffs of Harvard University's Houghton Library, the Massachusetts Historical Society and the Boston Athenaeum. Melanie Wisner, at the Houghton, was especially helpful as were Donald Yacovone and Brenda Lawson, at MHS.

Thanks to scholars Sandra Shaw and Katherine Dhalle, both of whom provided facts and inspiration. Henry Dwight Sedgwick and the Reverend Robert Shaw Sturgis Whitman, both of whom are blood relatives of Shaw, pointed out important details about Shaw's life and the life and death of Shaw's wife Anna Haggerty.

For assistance in collecting illustrations, a special vote of thanks to Chris Steele, at MHS. Producer Freddie Fields was a key player in the rounding up of photographs taken during the filming of the motion picture *Glory*. Marcie Granata and Barbara Lakin at TriStar Pictures, Inc. were cheerful allies in the acquisition of these photographs. Since Freddie Fields and director Edward Zwick were scrupulously accurate in reproducing uniforms and ordnance, the photographs are an important contribution to this book.

PREFACE

This book begins with what almost everyone agrees was the most important demonstration of the bravery of black soldiers in the American Civil War. In an editorial published five months after the war ended, the New York *Tribune* expressed what has become an accepted view of the importance of this episode.

> It is not too much to say that if the Massachusetts Fifty Fourth had faltered when its trial came, two hundred thousand colored troops for whom it was a pioneer would never have been put into the field, or would not have been put in for another year, which would have been equivalent to protracting the war into 1866. But it did not falter. It made Fort Wagner such a name to the colored race as Bunker Hill has been for ninety years to the white Yankees.

The physical and moral courage of black Americans had been proven many times before the attack by the Fifty Fourth Massachusetts Regiment on Fort Wagner—an earthwork that was part of a network of forts and batteries guarding Charleston, South Carolina—but such bravery had been repeatedly, sometimes willfully, ignored. Black men had fought courageously in the American Revolution and the War of 1812. In the Civil War, in coastal regions of the South, contrabands— escaped or abandoned slaves—who served in the First and Second South Carolina Volunteers had performed efficiently in raids on Confederate territory but had not engaged in major battles. Not long before the Fifty Fourth attacked Fort Wagner, black men loyal to the Union had displayed extraordinary bravery in the Mississippi River Valley—at Port Hudson and Milliken's Bend—but it remained for Colonel Robert Gould Shaw and his officers and men to demonstrate, beyond a shadow of a doubt, that African-Americans were capable of rising, with fire in their hearts, to fight for their rights as citizens and the freedom of their brothers.

On March 2, 1863, issuing a call to black men to join the Fifty Fourth, the great black abolitionist Frederick Douglass said, "The day dawns—the morning star is bright upon the horizon! The iron gate of our prison stands half open. One gallant rush from the North will fling it wide open, while four millions of our brothers and sisters shall march out into liberty!"

The men of the Fifty Fourth did indeed fling the gate wide open. Official records indicate that 178,975 black enlisted men and 7,122 officers—very few of whom were black—served in black Union regiments. These men fought in countless minor skirmishes and 39 major battles. Just under 10 percent of all soldiers who fought for the Union in the Civil War were African-Americans. More than 37,000 perished while in service. Some fell in battle, others succumbed to sicknesses that were fatal in a time when medicine was in its infancy.

The trouble with most general histories of the Civil War is that they treat it as a purely military conflict when, in fact, it was rooted in an overwhelming moral issue. For at least 100 years, general histories all but ignored black presence in the Union forces. At best, this presence, this participation, was presented as an unimportant footnote to the history of the war.

A distinguished Civil War historian—writing in the 1960s— expressed the convoluted view that a beneficial side effect of black enlistment in the Union armies was that it reduced the black population in the cities of the North and so reduced the social pressures that had led to what amounted to race riots. This view, aired in a supposedly enlightened century, is on a par with the notion that all black Americans should be returned to Africa, and it ignores the direct and positive effect of the participation of black Americans in what became their own crusade.

It took a major motion picture and an important television series to prompt large numbers of Americans to take a second look at the role of black men in a war that redefined the Constitution and began the reshaping of America.

Glory, which is largely fictional and sometimes misleading, is indisputably a powerful and affecting motion picture. I know two distinguished scholars who were outraged by it, but I know at least a dozen scholars of the period who loved and defended

Glory. In articles and reviews, it was almost universally admired. No less a Civil War historian than James M. McPherson praised the work.

> It is not only the first feature film to treat the role of black soldiers in the American Civil War; it is also the most powerful and historically accurate movie about the war ever made.

In general, *Glory* is indeed accurate. Its worst flaw is that it misrepresents the character of the young colonel who, one way or another, is its hero. In *Glory,* Shaw is represented as a weak and sometimes fumbling officer who employed a tough Irish sergeant to take over basic training of his men. In fact, Shaw was never weak and he was in command from first to last and, above all, he was just and never cruel. Though they appear in Chapter 5, a few lines from a letter Shaw wrote to his mother bear repeating in this foreword. They were written as Shaw shaped the regiment.

> One trouble that I have anticipated has begun: namely, complaints from outsiders of undue severity; but I shall continue to do what is right in that particular, and you may be perfectly certain that any reports of cruelty are entirely untrue.

History has the power to embitter people, but it has the power to ennoble them as well. Let us hope that greater knowledge of the vital roles played by black men and black women in the history of their country will ennoble all Americans. I have never thought that shoddy means should be excused, however noble are the ends, but if an imperfect motion picture has prompted a completion, or at least a correction, of the record of the Civil War, it should be celebrated by us all.

The television series I referred to earlier was, of course, the Ken Burns 11-hour documentary *The Civil War,* which followed *Glory,* in which Burns gave ample footage to the role played by black Americans.

—PETER BURCHARD
Williamstown, Massachusetts
1993

1

IN THE VANGUARD
July 18, 1863

On the evening of July 18, 1863, the soldiers of the Fifty Fourth gathered on a narrow strip of sand on Morris Island, one of a vast chain of islands strung along South Carolina's coastal plain.

The Fifty Fourth, child of Massachusetts Governor John A. Andrew, was the first black regiment formed since the issuance of the Emancipation Proclamation, the first recruited in the North. It was made up mostly of free men and was backed enthusiastically by crusaders of both races who, for more than 30 years, had been working tirelessly to eradicate the stain of slavery from their land.

For several days, Robert Gould Shaw, the young colonel of the regiment, had been struggling with a presentiment of death. Not long before, he had told his friend and second-in-command Lieutenant Colonel Edward N. Hallowell, "Oh Ned! If I could live a few weeks longer . . . and be home a little while I think I might die happy. But it cannot be. I do not believe I will live through our next fight."

Shaw turned toward the sea. A heavy mist was gathering above the deep. The sky was dark yet luminous, the ocean sullen and forbidding. Cresting waves marched toward the beach, white as baptismal raiments, hovered over by flights of small sea birds. For a moment, Shaw seemed lost in thought then, having come to terms with fate, he turned and walked among his men, smiling now and then at a familiar face, sometimes reaching out to touch the stiff uniform material of a sleeve or a shoulder.

He was only 25 but, in his final hour, he moved with the self-assurance of an older man. The son of abolitionists, he was firm in his resolve to lead his soldiers in what was to be a signal test of black Americans. He spoke softly, to one man, then another, his voice barely audible above the sound of the breaking of the waves on the sands, of the whisper and the hiss of the advancing and retreating waters.

The black men of the Fifty Fourth had been recruited far and wide, in all the Northern states, as far west as Illinois, and some in Canada. Most of them had been born free, but there were some who had been slaves in the Carolinas and Louisiana. Fewer than might have been expected had been laborers or servants. Waiting with Shaw and his officers were printers, barbers, seamen, blacksmiths, mechanics, harnessmakers, masons, teamsters, carpenters, cabinetmakers, farmers, upholsterers, shoemakers, musicians, dentists and bricklayers. Several stood out from the others. Tall, handsome First Sergeant Robert Simmons, born in Bermuda, lived in a New York City tenement with his mother, sister and two nephews. Lantern-jawed Sergeant Peter Vogelsang, recruited by Shaw's father in New York, was a steady sober man, the oldest in the regiment, almost a paternal figure, who had fought like a veteran in a skirmish on James Island. George E. Stephens, who had served in Virginia as a correspondent for the *Weekly Anglo African,* had joined the Fifty Fourth in January and had helped recruit men for the regiment. Sergeant William Carney, a seaman from New Bedford, Massachusetts, was young, slight of build, quick and cheerful, soon to become a hero.

While the regiment had waited for transport to Morris Island, Sergeant Simmons had written a short letter to his family. Referring to his first engagement, he said in part, "God has protected me through my first fiery leaden trial, and I do give him the glory, and render praises unto his holy name." He closed, "God bless you all! Goodbye!"

Though Shaw's family lived on Staten Island—5 miles or so southwest of New York City—and Hallowell's in Philadelphia, both men had roots in Massachusetts. In fact, most of Shaw's officers were natives of New England, many of them born to privilege. All were above what Governor Andrew called, ". . . a vulgar contempt for color." Among his officers, Shaw was especially fond of Hallowell, 19-year-old Captain Cabot Russel

This photograph was taken during the filming of the motion picture Glory. *It depicts a reenactment of the march of the Fifty Fourth toward Fort Wagner.* (Courtesy of Tristar Pictures, Inc.)

and Captain William Simkins, who had helped recruit men for the Fifty Fourth.

Every man who served in the regiment was aware that if he were captured he probably would not be treated with the courtesy accorded other prisoners of war. An officer commanding black men might be executed for inciting servile insurrection, while a free enlisted man or a fugitive from slavery might be shot, sold into bondage or returned to slavery.

A regiment should stand 1,000 strong, but sickness, death and the necessity of leaving a detachment of camp guards on St. Helena had depleted the ranks of the Fifty Fourth. That night, Shaw was to command 600 men, men short of sleep, who had had little food since morning, who were shy of drinking water and, most important, had engaged in their first hand-to-hand combat only two days earlier and afterward had marched in driving rain across a swamp and crossed a tidal inlet in unstable, leaking boats. Shaw himself had eaten only crackers for two days.

Shaw was blond. His skin was fair and was often pink from exposure to the elements but now, even as the setting sun touched and warmed the sand hills and salt marshes, his face was white as chalk. As he moved along the line, the men of his regiment reflected his affectionate regard for them. Some nodded firmly as he passed and others glanced admiringly at him.

Shaw approached Hallowell, who was talking to Shaw's adjutant, Garth James—brother of William James and Henry James, the first of whom was to become a teacher and philosopher and the other a distinguished novelist. As Shaw moved toward Hallowell and James, he turned to glance at the familiar silhouette of the regiment's objective. Fort Wagner, standing in the gloom several thousand yards from Shaw's position, was an enormous earthwork, some said the strongest ever built. Constructed of turf and quartz sand, reenforced by huge palmetto logs—whole trees felled just above the high-water mark—it was known to be armed with 15 guns, including five howitzers. There were no soldiers visible on the fort, but the Confederate flag flapped and fluttered on its pole.

Having been under fire, the fort was almost shapeless now, seeming little more than a monstrous mound of sand and earth, dark against the ragged clouds that were drifting high above Fort Sumter, which stood guard above a ships' channel that bisected a sandbar. The dredged passage was the gateway to a bay and harbor, to the rivers on the flanks of the meandering peninsula where the spires of Charleston rose high above the rooftops of the beautiful beleaguered city—seen in the North as a symbol of rebellion.

All day long, Fort Wagner had been shelled by the cannon of a siege line just north of Shaw's position and by the guns of a U.S. Navy squadron, standing offshore, out of range of the Confederate batteries, some of which were on the northern tip of Morris Island and were shielded by the fort. Other forts and gun emplacements were ranged around Charleston's harbor and its waterways, protecting mooring grounds and docks that gave refuge to varieties of fast ships whose captains knew how to navigate in darkness, how to knife through the blockade of important Southern ports.

Shaw's brigade commander, young and attractive General Strong, was acquainted with Fort Wagner. A week before, he had led an attack on the stronghold and had been driven back, but he believed that the earthwork had been devastated by today's bombardment, that now it could be taken by direct assault. He estimated that no more than 300 hundred men were in the fort.

Strong knew that Shaw's men, in their initial contact with the enemy on James Island, had not only proved themselves but had saved a company of the Tenth Connecticut from annihilation. Even so, it was only at Shaw's urging and at the insistence of his men that Strong and General Seymour, who commanded the assault, had agreed to let the Fifty Fourth show the way, and both men had warned Shaw that his losses might be heavy.

As it happened, Strong was wrong about the condition of the fort and the disposition of its men. The soldiers of its garrison had spent the day relaxing, sometimes sleeping, in a bombproof shelter just behind the southeast bastion of the work. There were 1,700 of them. Moreover, the Confederate gunners had built barricades that had protected their artillery. Not a single piece had been so much as scratched. In fact, the bombardment had done little more than stiffen the resolve of the defending soldiers.

Shaw heard the sound of hoofbeats on the sand. Strong appeared, mounted on a great gray charger, with a yellow kerchief at his neck, riding with two orderlies. In ringing tones, he addressed the members of Fifty Fourth. "I am sorry that you must go into battle tired and hungry, but the men in the fort are tired too. . . . Go in and bayonet them at their guns." Gesturing toward the young flag bearer who held the stars and stripes, he asked, "If this man should fall, who will lift the flag and carry it on?"

Shaw's raised his voice. "I will," he said.

George Stephens noted that, without dishonoring himself, a man of Shaw's rank could have marched behind his men. "He did not take his thirty paces to the rear. . . ."

When Shaw promised to pick up the flag, if the flag bearer fell, it was clear that he intended to go first. A shout went up from the throat of every soldier in the regiment, rising, echoing and dying. At least one Confederate soldier must have heard the sound. It was followed shortly by the defiant crack of a single rifle shot.

That afternoon, Shaw had engaged in a solemn conversation with a man named Edward Pierce—a friend of his parents who had headed a program to educate abandoned slaves, had been active in recruiting soldiers for the Fifty Fourth and was working now as a correspondent for the New York *Tribune*. Now Shaw went to Pierce and asked him to take special note of the bravery of his men. He handed Pierce some letters to be given to his wife and his parents if he were killed or captured. Then, left alone with Hallowell, Shaw spoke again as a man who might not see another dawn. Although he knew that Hallowell would follow closely after him as they approached the fort, it seems not to have occurred to him that his lieutenant colonel might be killed. He gave Hallowell some verbal messages for his young wife, his parents and his sisters. Then he told him that if he fell in battle he wanted to make sure that one of his good horses be presented to Charlotte Forten—a young black woman from the North who was working as a teacher of the children of abandoned slaves.

As Shaw and his men waited for the signal to attack Fort Wagner, Abraham Lincoln and his supporters had begun to hope for victory in a war that was then in progress in a vast territory—in the South, East and West. The battle at Antietam Creek, in Maryland, in which Shaw had taken part as a captain in the Second Massachusetts Regiment, had been a draw but had been seen by Lincoln as a turning point. The greatest battle of the war, at Gettysburg, had taken place two weeks earlier and had been followed by the withdrawal of the Confederate forces.

Only 10 days after Gettysburg, misguided men in a great Northern city had joined together in a kind of barbarism that made a mockery of the Emancipation Proclamation and of the humanity and sacrifice of more than 40,000 young Americans—Northerners and Southerners—who had been killed or wounded in that Pennsylvania town. For four days—July 13 to 16—unknown to the soldiers of the Fifty Fourth, New York City had been the scene of riots brought on partly by a law that allowed a man to avoid conscription by paying a substitute to take his place. An enormous mob of laborers, made up of men enraged by the injustice of this law, attacked and seized an armory and began a bloody rampage. Instead of taking out their anger on the legislators who had drafted the Conscription Act, the rioters directed their activities at blacks and known abolitionists. They beat black citizens to death, shot others and, in some cases, dragged their bodies through the streets and strung them up in public places.

Mercifully, Sergeant Simmons had been spared the tragic news that his seven-year-old nephew—described as a gentle boy who was in some way handicapped—had been stoned to death on the street where he lived, killed by a gang of grown men who hated blacks.

Shaw knew that this latest move against Charleston, if successful, would help tighten the blockade, thus preventing Southern troops from receiving arms and ammunition from the British. He knew that the war had started here, on April 12, 1861, with the firing on Fort Sumter, knew that to render Charleston helpless would be to deal a mortal blow to the morale of the Confederacy and would reenforce the impression that the North was on the way to victory but, above all, he knew that the Fifty Fourth must play an even more important role in his country's history and in the lives of black Americans.

Though he was born and raised an abolitionist, Shaw had at times rebelled against his parents' single-mindedness, but he had never turned his back on their crusade. Serving in the Second Massachusetts, he had shown keen interest in the recruiting of black regiments but, as commander of the pioneering Fifty Fourth, he became at least as single-minded as his parents. In fact, since Shaw had decided to accept command of the Fifty Fourth, he had known that if he wavered once he would be disgraced and that he would bring down with him the hopes and aspirations of a whole race of people.

As the twilight deepened, the silence in the fort was broken now and then by the boom of Confederate cannon. When a shot passed overhead, one of Shaw's men stirred, recoiling nervously, and Hallowell spoke sharply to him. Thinking of the Confederates in the fort, another soldier whispered, "I guess they kind of 'spec's we're coming."

Having given Hallowell his message, Shaw, who was wearing a close-fitting jacket with a silver eagle on each shoulder, moved again among his men, who were formed in battle lines but not standing at attention. Walking calmly down the line, he told them that they must prove themselves. One remembered that he said, "The eyes of thousands will look on what you do tonight." Hallowell wrote later that a slight twitching at the corners of Shaw's mouth revealed, ". . . that the whole cost was counted."

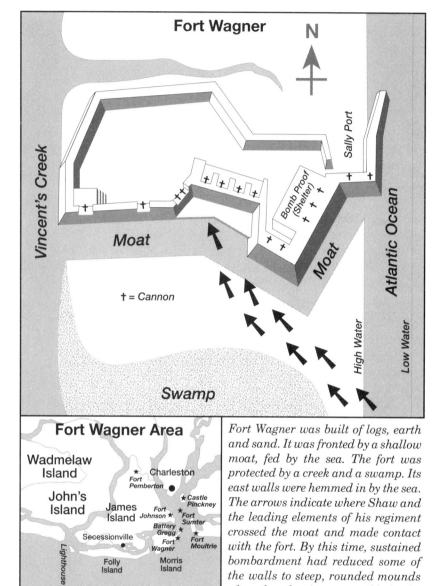

Fort Wagner

N

Vincent's Creek

Sally Port

Atlantic Ocean

Bomb Proof (Shelter)

Moat

Moat

High Water

Low Water

† = Cannon

Swamp

Fort Wagner Area

Wadmelaw Island

John's Island

James Island

Secessionville

Folly Island

Morris Island

Lighthouse Inlet

Charleston

Fort Pemberton

Castle Pinckney

Fort Johnson

Fort Sumter

Battery Gregg

Fort Wagner

Fort Moultrie

Fort Wagner was built of logs, earth and sand. It was fronted by a shallow moat, fed by the sea. The fort was protected by a creek and a swamp. Its east walls were hemmed in by the sea. The arrows indicate where Shaw and the leading elements of his regiment crossed the moat and made contact with the fort. By this time, sustained bombardment had reduced some of the walls to steep, rounded mounds of sand so that it was possible for the attackers to scale the parapet.

A ghostly courier, on a bay horse, brought Shaw the order to advance. Shaw pocketed the paper, stood erect, slid the holster holding his revolver to the front of his jacket and deliberately unsheathed his sword. Calling his men to order, he paused a moment, then shouted, "Forward march!"

The beach ahead was hemmed in sharply by the ocean on the right and tidal creeks and salt marshes on the left. The tide was rising, having turned three hours earlier, forcing the men on the right to wade in shallow water. Every soldier taking part in the attack knew that Wagner was protected by a moat that was flooded by the sea. All knew that, as they approached the southeast bastion, they would be forced, by the sea and the marshlands, to move into a bottleneck, where they would face concentrated rifle fire before they could hope to wade the moat, scale the wall and occupy the fort. It was understood that there would be no time to pause and fire, that they must engage their enemy in hand-to-hand combat.

As Shaw began to march, the way grew ever narrower. Close to him, were the two color-bearers, one with the stars and stripes and the other with the Massachusetts state flag—a snow-white field with a shield in its center. A steady wind made the banners flutter constantly.

The guns of the batteries behind Fort Wagner at the north end of the island and the guns of Fort Sumter and several other forts started to bombard the forward elements of the assaulting column. Now and then, Shaw turned and told a junior officer or a sergeant to keep the ranks in order but, when he saw the dark shapes of the men on his right marching knee-deep in the surf, he knew that the advance was to be disorderly. He must have understood that, if the southeast bastion was manned by skillful riflemen, the attack would be costly if not completely futile.

As the transparent light of evening gave way to the dark of night, Shaw's men kept following the flags. Suddenly the great prow of the southeast bastion rose up in front of them, black against the deep night sky. A Confederate officer gave a shout and then it was as if the fort exploded. One of Shaw's officers remembered later, "A sheet of flame, followed by a running fire, like electric sparks, swept along the parapet."

As it happened, a North Carolina regiment had failed to take its place in the southeast bastion but, even so, the artillery fire that poured forth from the fort was so intense that men all around Shaw were struck—twisting in a dance of agony, a dance of death. Shaw shouted, quickening his pace, and led the flag bearers and survivors toward the moat.

The repeated boom of cannon, the crackle of a thousand muskets and the sight of fallen comrades might have made lesser men cut and run but no man of the Fifty Fourth paused, checked or retreated. The pulsing light of cannon fire illuminated gaping holes in the ground and the fort made by Union guns that afternoon. As the flash of continuing explosions blinded the invaders, some stumbled into shell holes, crawled out and moved onward.

In the intermittent light, Shaw ran toward the moat. Later, Hallowell remembered, "I saw him again, just for an instant, as he sprang into the ditch. His broken and shattered regiment were following him. . . ." Shaw plunged into the salty waters, legs churning, body bent. Behind him, the man who held the stars and stripes was disabled. Sergeant Carney grasped the pole, raised the flag and fought forward, catching up with his commander and the man who held the Massachusetts flag. The three men led the survivors up the massive wall of earth and sand, slipping, sliding but advancing into concentrated musket fire, while the wounded and the dead pitched backward down the slope.

At last, Shaw stood on the parapet and, in a momentary lull, his voice rang out, clear and strong. The man who carried the state flag was shot and killed. The men who followed Shaw saw their commander etched against the smoke and flame, his bright sword pointing toward the heavens. He hung, suspended, for a instant, then crumpled and fell forward.

2

BOYHOOD AND YOUTH
1837–60

Why did a young white man, having everything to live for, join with black Americans, sometimes to suffer vicious prejudice, often to endure what he called ". . . sneering and pitying remarks . . . " and, at last, to lead his brothers in a desperate charge against what turned out to be an impregnable earthwork?

Part of the answer to this question can be found in Shaw's background. He was born in Boston, Massachusetts, on October 10, 1837. His parents—Francis George Shaw and Sarah Blake Sturgis Shaw—were members of rich and aristocratic families. Both were descended from early colonists—Francis Shaw from land speculator John Shaw and Sarah Shaw from Elias Parkman, a merchant and fur trader.

Shaw's great-great uncle, Major Samuel Shaw, was aide-de-camp to Major General Henry Knox, who commanded George Washington's artillery in important battles in the revolutionary war. Major Shaw became the first American to engage in trade with China. In 1784, he sailed as business agent on the *Empress of China,* to Canton. He traded mostly ginseng root—found in New England and used as medicine by the Chinese—and came home in 1785, with spices, teas and silks.

As Major Shaw, and other Boston merchants and their Salem brethren, built ever-faster clipper ships and sailed them around Cape Horn to Asian ports, engaging in what was called the China trade, they brought untold wealth and power to themselves and to their families. Historian Samuel Eliot Morison wrote, "Boston was the Spain, Salem the Portugal in the race for Oriental opulence."

Continued wise investment, in real estate, railroads and manufacturing, made the Shaws and other Boston families so rich that their sons and daughters could abandon commerce altogether. Shaw's parents were among those few Bostonians who used their financial independence to write and speak, sometimes to act, against the scourge of slavery and, in so doing, found themselves ridiculed by their peers, most of whom were, in one way or another, making money from slave labor, which fed cotton to the looms of Massachusetts and provided Northern merchants with rice and tobacco.

Until Shaw was five, he and his family lived at 53 Bowdoin Street, on a slope of Beacon Hill, in a house whose brick exterior concealed great luxury. The parlor, dining room and halls sheltered many treasures of the China trade—silk hangings, exquisite lacquerware, carved objects of ivory, porcelain and jade, and teakwood furniture. In the house were living quarters for a staff of servants—cooks, maids, coachmen, grooms. In back, with access to an alleyway, was a stable that contained stalls for the horses and accommodations for a carriage.

It was into such a world that Shaw was born. In childhood, he was extraordinary looking. He was smaller than his playmates and his golden hair framed a high forehead. He had a firm but generous mouth. His eyes were his most compelling feature. They were dark blue and sometimes betrayed a hint of melancholy. He was a lively and sometimes rebellious child who relished the companionship of children his own age but clung tenaciously to the members of his family.

His parents and his older sister Anna loved him deeply, though each in an entirely different way. They called him Rob. Francis Shaw was a gentle, balding man with a full beard and clear blue eyes. Even as Rob grew up, his father retired from business to become a reformer and a scholar. He studied social theories and believed deeply in the rights of ordinary people. No doubt Rob's father—whose activities had their roots in long-considered, deeply held social beliefs—had much to do with his son's capacity to change from a fun-loving youth to a dedicated man.

Francis Shaw responded to Rob's sensitive but independent spirit, which he found both admirable and touching. He spent many hours with his son, at first on Boston Common and in the Public Garden.

As Rob became sure-footed, man and child toured the city, walking up Beacon Hill, to admire the gilded State House dome, going sometimes downhill to the waterfront. They must have stood at the foot of India Wharf—headquarters of Russell and Company, owned by Russells, Forbeses, Crowninshields, all related to the Shaws—while Francis Shaw explained the importance of the wharf to the fortunes of their family.

Rob's mother was a force against which he rebelled throughout his childhood and his youth. She had a strong nose and a determined chin. She made it known that her health was constantly in question, but it is clear that some of her illnesses were contrived. As a boy in boarding school, he would tell her, "I don't want to write every week, it's too much trouble . . . if you think I'm sick when I don't write, you can send for me to come and tell you."

Later, as a fledgling soldier, he was to protest her invasion of his privacy.

> I can't see any solid reason for sending a private letter to a newspaper . . . I shouldn't object half so much if the extracts were practically anonymous but it is always perfectly evident to all my acquaintances that I wrote them, and I am at this moment in a state of high anxiety about what Father has had printed. It is the very last thing *he* would like, I know. The fact is I can't write what I want if my letters are to be put in the papers.

Anna doted on her little brother. Rob returned her affection and, in turn, was to take a gentle and protective attitude toward his three younger sisters—Susanna, Josephine and Ellen.

In the vastness of America, most of which was thinly populated, Boston was an extraordinary city. Alexis de Tocqueville, a bright young French nobleman who traveled in America with his friend Gustave de Beaumont just before Rob was born, likened Boston to great European capitals. Of Boston's aristocracy, he wrote, "Society, at least the society in which we have been introduced, and I think that is the first, resembles almost completely the upper classes in Europe. Their manners are distinguished, their conversation turns on intellectual matters. . . . " In Boston, Tocqueville talked to John Quincy Adams, the small hawk-eyed son of the Union's second president and himself its sixth president. Tocqueville asked him, "Do you look on slavery as a great plague for the United States?"

"Yes. Certainly," Adams answered. "That is the root of almost all the troubles of the present and fears for the future."

Even the opinions of so distinguished an American as John Quincy Adams carried very little weight with most of Boston's merchant-princes but, against all their money and their power, were arrayed a small and courageous band of abolitionists who saw that slavery and democracy couldn't live in the same nation. As Shaw's parents joined a new generation of crusaders in what at first was a nonviolent movement, one of their most effective leaders was William Lloyd Garrison, who started his heroic work during the 1820s—a time when most people in the North were indifferent to the fate of slaves.

In his early days in Boston, Garrison, who had come from Newburyport—a seaport north of Boston—was very poor. When he was in his early twenties, he lived in a rooming house, slept sometimes in his office with his cat that, a friend remembered, ". . . caressed his bald forehead in a most affectionate way." As a young man, Garrison sometimes sustained himself on a slice of bread, an apple and a glass of water.

Garrison not only changed the course of many lives but changed the course of history. A Boston woman said of him, "he it was who created, almost single-handed, the moral force which overthrew slavery."

Garrison was small-boned, sharp-featured and energetic. At first, he expressed his views in letters—to *The Salem Gazette, The Newburyport Herald* and *The Boston Courier* —then began to lecture widely.

In general, abolitionists saw Independence Day celebrations as an absurdity. On July 4, 1829, when he was only 24, Garrison stood in the pulpit of Boston's Park Street Church and made the first of many speeches against slavery.

As he began, he peered intently at his audience through oval steel-rimmed spectacles. He spoke of the Declaration of Independence, signed 53 years earlier. He said that the day of the signing of the document, ". . . shook as with a great earthquake, thrones which were seemingly propped up with Atlantean pillars." Having demonstrated to his audience the importance of the great declaration, he expressed dismay that freedom gained for white Americans in the revolutionary war had not been extended to all black Americans. As he warmed to his thesis, he quoted Cicero, who had lived and spoken almost 2,000 years before. "It is not possible for the people of Rome to be slaves, whom the gods have destined to command all nations. Other nations may endure slavery, but the proper end and business of the Roman people is liberty!"

Garrison appealed directly to the conscience of the North, asserting that the free states must bear part of the guilt attached to slavery, ". . . by adhering to a national compact that sanctions it." He insisted that it was the duty of the North to assist in overthrowing it. Of the United States, he declared, "If the blood of souls is on her garments yet she heeds not the stains."

A month later, Garrison went down to Baltimore where he worked with itinerant Quaker abolitionist Benjamin Lundy, to publish a weekly antislavery paper, *The Genius of Emancipation.* All went well until, in an editorial, Garrison attacked a fellow Yankee for transporting 88 slaves from Baltimore to New Orleans and was accused of libel. Garrison's charge was true but he was convicted. In jail seven weeks, he had time for reflection and for writing and decided he would publish his own paper.

Released from jail on June 5, 1830, Garrison moved to Boston where, on January 1, 1831, with his partner Isaac Knapp, he published the first issue of *The Liberator.* This paper was to continue to appear until 1865, when slavery was at last outlawed in the United States. His first declaration in the paper was, "I am in earnest—I will not equivocate—I will not excuse—I will not retreat a single inch—*and I will be heard.*" From the start, *The Liberator* took an uncompromising stand for immediate and unconditional abolition of slavery—the institution called by Garrison, ". . . the vampire which is feeding on our life's blood." The newspaper wasn't widely read, but it was quoted widely, and a single issue had the power of a stick of dynamite. It enraged the people of the South and hardened their determination to create new states that would vote with it in supporting slavery where it stood and support the spread of slavery.

Though he had frequently declared himself nonviolent, Garrison was himself subjected to brutality. On October 21, 1835, he was mobbed because he was a guest at a meeting of the Boston Female Anti-Slavery Society. He was seized by his enemies and dragged into State Street, where a rope was tied around his body and the clothes torn from his back. Witnesses reported later that he showed no fear whatsoever and, perhaps more important, neither he nor his supporters answered brutality with violence. At least one member of the mob suggested hanging Garrison but, at last, he was rescued by Mayor Theodore Lyman, Jr. and his officers and put in jail so he would be safe until his attackers left the neighborhood.

The Shaws were among the first to join Garrison's crusade and, once committed, they were among his most persistent followers. Rob was sometimes to grow tired of antislavery talk and at times rebelled against the idea that he must become an extension of his parents' beliefs.

An only son, Rob was pampered. He wore tailored clothes and, now and then, at teatime, was shepherded through the doorways of great houses on the streets, squares and narrow alleys on the crest and on the slopes of Beacon Hill. Later, he expressed his dislike of "cussed teaparties" but, as a child, he was forced to endure them. At these exclusive gatherings, however, he did meet many of his mother's brilliant colleagues.

Indeed, Sarah Shaw had many loyal and admiring friends among American and British abolitionists. There were as many women abolitionists as there were men. Women's voices often rose to express a degree of passion seen in only the most dedicated men. While these women wrote and spoke against the shame of slavery, they also pressed their struggle for the right to vote and campaigned against intemperance. First among Sarah Shaw's friends was successful novelist Lydia Maria Child. Many less-accomplished women, in defiance of their merchant husbands, joined the Female Anti-Slavery Society. In Boston, in the 19th century, this kind of defiance was tantamount to mutiny.

As a child, Rob went often to his mother's family's house at 44 Beacon Street. The walls of this house were decorated with seascapes and landscapes painted by Chinese artists and with family portraits executed by distinguished painters, among them Gilbert Stuart, who had done three portraits of George Washington.

When Rob was five, his family moved from Boston to a pleasant country house in West Roxbury surrounded by rolling hills, open fields, stone walls, unpaved country roads and small patches of woodland. The Shaws lived close to Brook Farm, a utopian community, where scientists, musicians, artists, novelists, poets and philosophers lived together, shared their fortunes and worked for the good of all. Brook Farm was ridiculed by conservative Bostonians, but good poetry and literary criticism was written by some of its inhabitants.

Rob's father was described by a neighbor as, "... a very kind friend of the Brook Farmers." Dr. John Thomas Codman, who wrote a history of Brook Farm, remembered that Francis Shaw, "... on his horse, with his young son, a tiny little fellow, on a pony by his side, often galloped over to the Farm to call."

In West Roxbury, the Shaws became parishioners of Theodore Parker, one of several ministers who preached and wrote against the sin of slavery. Like Garrison, he had sprung from humble origins. He and his wife lived in a cottage. His Spring Street Memorial Church looked like many other country churches in New England. It was painted white, topped by a simple steeple, screened by a row of elms.

Parker was 32 when Shaw's family joined his congregation. He was a zealous patriot, a scholar who commanded 20 languages, a man who used his broad education to give substance to his abolitionism. When he preached, he minced no words, asserting that any man or woman, black or white, had a right, if not a duty, to kill anyone who sought to rob him or her of liberty. "The man who attacks me to reduce me to slavery, in that moment of attack alienates his right to life, and if I were the fugitive, and could escape in no other way, I would kill him with as little compunction as I would drive a mosquito from my face."

Even when he was a boy, Rob was made to feel that he must share in his family's obligations. He was named for his paternal grandfather and, when the elder Shaw was dying, he went to visit him with another grandson, Henry Sturgis Russell. Their grandfather looked at the two boys and said, "My children, I am leaving the stage of action and you are entering upon it. I exhort you to use your example and influence against intemperance and slavery."

When Shaw was nine, his family moved to West New Brighton, New York—on Staten Island—so Shaw's mother, who had an eye ailment, could be attended by Samuel McKenzie Elliot, an eminent Scots specialist who lived and practiced there. By then, New York and Boston seemed much closer to each other than they had not long before, when the journey, on the old

Boston Post Road, had been arduous, sometimes taking more than two days and involving many stops. In Shaw's youth, in all but the coldest winter months, a traveler could leave Boston at teatime, go by train to Providence, Rhode Island, board a steamer, eat supper, bed down in a comfortable stateroom and arrive in New York's East River at 11:00 in the morning, having had a good night's sleep and a satisfying breakfast.

When Shaw moved there, Staten Island was as rural as West Roxbury. Much of the land was farmed, while some of it was taken up by large estates occupied by sons and daughters of some of New York's richest families. The Shaws lived in a large house high on a hill, overlooking Kill Van Kull—a tidal channel on the north side of the island. On clear days, the house commanded a broad view of New York Bay and the steeples of the city, which rose high above the stone and red brick downtown buildings. At night, a lighthouse on nearby Robbins Reef flashed its signal on the bedroom ceilings.

At first, he was sent to a small private school on Staten Island, then went to a boarding school—St. John's College Roman Catholic School at Fordham, 20 miles or so from Staten Island. Though most members of Rob's family were Unitarians, his uncle Coolidge Shaw had joined the Jesuit order and had urged that his nephew be subjected to the discipline found in a school run by his fellow Jesuits.

Though he was separated from his family by no more than a two-hour journey—by railroad and ferry—Rob was desperately homesick. He hated his schoolmaster who, as was the custom then, struck his students with a ruler or a cane when they were disobedient and often doled out punishments for crimes not committed. In a letter to his parents, he expressed his desperation. "I'd rather do anything than stay here for I don't want to be whipped unjustly, and I won't stand it." He wrote to his parents often. In one of his early letters, he beseeched, "I do wish you would come and see me right off, and not wait so long as Christmas, for I feel very homesick. . . . I can hardly help crying when I am writing this note."

Some of Shaw's schoolmates were cruel. He reported, "This morning a big black cat got into the study room, and the boys yelled and screamed like anything. They were all standing up on their desks and firing books and sticks at the poor cat, which kept jumping at the windows, and climbing up the woodwork of the walls; at last one of the boys hit it on the head with a big stick and killed it."

The atmosphere at Fordham so depressed young Shaw that he thought of running off with a friend, who had himself run away once before, to work aboard a Hudson River sloop—a large sailboat used as a cargo vessel—but winter was setting in and Shaw chose instead to go home without permission. His father didn't punish him but took him back. A week later, Shaw wrote, "If they had whipped me then, I am almost certain I should have run away again, I should have been so mad."

When he was 10, he left Fordham and sailed to Europe with his family. He spent six months with his family, studying and traveling, and in the fall of 1851 went to school in Neuchatel, Switzerland, a town surrounded by snow-covered mountain peaks. His school was presided over by Monsieur and Madame Roulet. He loved the place and admired Roulet so much that, all his life, he carried a small photograph of him with those of members of his own family.

Shaw had little use for scholarship, unless he saw how it might be applied, but Monsieur Roulet was an inspiring teacher, and Shaw learned some mathematics, chemistry and geology. He began to speak and read French and German, took violin lessons and read poetry and contemporary novels. Much as he liked the Roulets, he chafed at the restrictions they imposed on him. Shaw, then and later, was persistent in his love of freedom. Later, serving in the military, he expressed his love of open spaces, choosing often to sleep on a blanket, in the open, looking upward at the stars. In Europe, he matured but displayed few of the sterling qualities that were to mark his character when he became a soldier.

Few people in their teens know how they want to spend their adult years. Shaw was no exception. He knew he didn't want to be a businessman, a lawyer or a doctor. His experience at Fordham made it unthinkable that he would embrace religion in any of its forms. In response to his mother's urging that he declare himself a Unitarian, he wrote, "I don't want to become a reformer, Apostle, or anything of that kind." He thought of going to the U.S. Military Academy, at West Point, but that seems to have been a passing fancy.

Shaw left Roulet's school in 1853, in September, and spent the following 10 months with his family in Sorrento, Italy.

Shaw in 1849, when he was 12. (The Houghton Library, Harvard University)

There, he met British-born actress Fanny Kemble, a friend of his parents. In one of her journals, Kemble described Sorrento. She wrote of palaces, ". . . built of marble, and rising out of orange groves, and commanding from every window, terrace and balcony, incomparable views of seas, shores and islands, renowned in history and poetry and lovelier than imagination."

Kemble probably talked to the Shaws about her experiences as the wife of Pierce Butler, Georgia's richest slaveowner. In any case, Shaw was destined to see part of Butler's vast plantation and to talk to people who had been his slaves.

In the spring of 1854, Shaw's family left him in Hanover, Germany, where he remained on his own for two years, continuing his education—much of it with private tutors—but concentrating mostly on amusements. He went to countless parties, drank more than his share of beer and wine and wrote often to his parents for more money.

Shaw made the most of Hanover—an ancient city on the Leine, with a charming market square, narrow streets and ornate houses. He went often to the opera and the theater and led an active social life. As he approached his 17th birthday, he wrote his mother, "You can't conceive how big inside I've gotten since I've been here. I'm at least five years older than when I came; but it is a natural consequence of being left alone and at my own disposition. I begin to find you treat me too *little* in your letters."

The most influential antislavery volume of its time was Harriet Beecher Stowe's *Uncle Tom's Cabin,* first published on March 20, 1852. Shaw read the novel several times. "I've been reading 'Uncle Tom's Cabin' again lately, and always like it better than before and see more things in it."

Uncle Tom was frankly propaganda; Shaw was familiar with many of its moral and religious arguments, but the book involved highly sympathetic characters and included powerful and convincing illustrations of the tragedy of slavery. Early in the narrative, there is a dialogue between a slave dealer and a Southern gentleman in financial trouble. Asked to sell the child of one of his young woman slaves, the gentleman says, "The fact is, sir, I'm a humane man, and I hate to take the boy from his mother, sir."

The slave dealer sympathizes. "I al'ays hates these screechin', screamin' times. They are *mighty* onpleasant but, as I manages business, I generally avoids 'em, sir. Now, what if you get the girl off for a day, or a week, or so; then the thing's done quietly—all over before she comes home. Your wife might get her some ear-rings, or a new gown or some such truck, to make up with her."

Later, when the mother, whose name is Eliza, hears that her little son is indeed to be sold, she escapes with him and is pursued by professional slave-catchers, one of whom talks about the danger of his dogs. "Our dogs tore a feller half to pieces once, down in Mobile, 'fore we could get 'em off."

The book swept America and the world. A year after publication, it had sold 305,000 copies in the United States and many times this number overseas. Here was something everyone who could read could understand. It spelled the doom of slavery. Stowe herself explained that, before her book appeared, slavery was widely thought of as a dangerous subject, that imagining oneself in the position of a slave would be, to say the least, unsettling. She wrote that, ". . . nobody could begin to read and think upon it without becoming practically insane." During the Civil War, Stowe was to pay a call on Abraham Lincoln, who looked down at her from his great height and said gently, "So this is the little lady who made this big war."

Stowe's book affected Shaw, as it had other readers, and it was about this time that his resistance to his parents' singlemindedness grew less intense. He read the New York *Daily Tribune,* which reported outrages against Northern blacks and Southern slaves. He read of an Alabama slave, accused of rape and murder, who was taken out of jail and burned alive. Fellow slaves were made to watch the ghastly execution. The accused may or may not have been guilty but, standing on a pile of wood, tied to a willow stake, he confessed just before the wood was fired. As he died, ". . . his black and burning carcass, like a demon of fire, grinned as if in hellish triumph at his tormentors."

In Hanover, Shaw dined and danced with young women. He especially admired the 14-year-old daughter of a friend of his and was to remember her, even after he left Europe. He traveled in Norway, with two of his student friends, riding through the countryside, sleeping in the huts and barns of country folk.

Shaw's family went back home in the spring of 1856 and, in August, Shaw followed after them, spent a week on Staten Island and then went north to attend Harvard University, in Cambridge, Massachusetts. In his day, Cambridge looked like a country village but was near enough to Boston so that students were attracted to the city's cabarets and hotels. Artemus Ward—a popular humorist of Shaw's time—reported that the college was, ". . . located in the Parker House bar." Today, entry into Harvard is an honor much sought after, but Shaw and his cousins and their friends took the college pretty much for granted. In fact, at first, he scorned the institution. He wrote that everything was, ". . . horridly stupid here and just like a school."

Established in 1636, it was the first institution of its kind in America. Named for John Harvard, who left some of his money and his library to the institution, it was started by high-minded men, mostly for the education of the gentry. Its charter, signed in 1650, specified that the college was to dedicate itself to the advancement of the knowledge of good literature, arts and sciences. By the time Shaw entered Harvard it was becoming a great modern university.

In Shaw's class at Harvard were several of his cousins and a number of his friends, some of whom were destined to serve with him in the Second Regiment of Massachusetts Volunteers. In college, the nearest thing to war was something called Bloody Monday, a day when the brutality of freshman initiation reached its peak. In his book *Three Centuries of Harvard,* Samuel Eliot Morison wrote, "The average freshman was literally afraid for his life at the beginning of the college year, for the sophomores took care to spread horrifying accounts of what would happen on the first Monday of the term." On Shaw's Bloody Monday, he and his fellow freshmen were told to wear white flannel trousers, blazers and straw hats and gather on a football field. There they were opposed by larger, more aggressive sophomores and their clothes torn to shreds. Shaw wrote, "After the first game, few had their own hats on, few had a whole shirt, and there were more black eyes, bloody noses and broken teeth than you could well count." Shaw was small and he was trampled. "That was Monday and today is Friday but my head has not got entirely well yet."

Shaw joined a boating club, played his violin in string quartets and went to social gatherings. In time, he grew almost fond of Cambridge, but he missed the footloose life he had led in Hanover. During his first year at Harvard, he thought often of the German girl who had so appealed to him. Now she was 17 and he thought of writing her, to ask for her hand in marriage, but time and distance had already dimmed his ardor. The sun was soon to shine on several young women in New York but, for awhile, he remained fancy-free and often went to skating parties, games and concerts with his sister Susie, who was a student at a boarding school in Cambridge. He went to see her in a Christmas play and wrote proudly to his parents, "Susie was really beautiful . . . everybody seemed to be looking at her, for I heard 'Susie Shaw' whispered all around me. . . . "

Shaw, like his father, studied botany and must have visited the Botanic Garden, Gray's Herbarium and the Arnold Arboretum, all of which were in existence during his student days, but he lost interest in his studies. He dreamed of adventure, was attracted to the stories of the western guides and pioneers and thought of settling in the West. He was so opposed to living out his life indoors that he wrote, "I had rather be a chimney sweep. . . . "

The financial panic of 1858 devastated many of Shaw's relatives but, though Shaw's parents' income was reduced, his family suffered few, if any, deprivations. He could certainly have stayed in college but he grew bored with Harvard and, thinking that a position in a firm involved in foreign trade might lead to travel, he jumped at an opportunity to work for his uncle Henry Sturgis, one of the titans of the China trade, a man who traveled almost constantly and commanded the respect of both Asians and Americans.

Sturgis had his offices in New York, and Shaw started working in the city in the spring of 1859, living mostly with his family on Staten Island. On the ferry going to and from Manhattan, he was treated to a view of New York's Upper Bay, which was constantly traversed by sailing vessels and steamships, some of which made extended voyages to distant lands. These sights increased his wanderlust and, when he saw that the job in his uncle's firm promised only office work, he grew depressed and fretful. A friend wrote to him, hoping he could go with him on a hunting expedition, and Shaw answered, "How I would like to go on that deer-hunt. But I am a slave now and, even if I were invited, I could not go."

3

TO THE DEFENSE OF WASHINGTON 1860–62

In the fall of 1860, as Lincoln's first presidential campaign swept into New York City—a key city in a state that he must capture if he was to win the election—Shaw took a lively interest in the contest, watching the processions move up and down Broadway, listening to the speeches in the parks and public buildings, talking to his parents, to his sisters and his friends, most of whom supported Lincoln.

On the whole, the campaign was serene. It was far less clamorous than the campaign of 1856, in which John Charles Fremont, the first Republican presidential candidate, was defeated. Considering the flaming issues facing the electorate in 1860, it is perhaps not surprising that the four candidates—Abraham Lincoln, Stephen Douglas, John C. Breckenridge and John Bell—talked about the issues, not about each other.

Shaw had heard from people who knew Lincoln that he was, ". . . a pure, honest-minded, patriotic man, and that whatever he did would be for the good of country." Massachusetts Governor John Andrew had met Lincoln at the Republican convention in Chicago and had seen, ". . . in a flash that here was a man who was master of himself. For the first time they [the delegates] understood that he whom they had supposed to be little more than a loquacious and clever politician, had force, insight, conscience, that their misgivings were in vain."

Lincoln, born in 1809, in Kentucky, had had few advantages, but his parents—poor but enlightened people—were opposed to slavery. There were slaves in the part of Kentucky where Lincoln spent his early childhood, but he had seen few, if any, of them. He long remembered a black woman servant who had given him a glass of milk while his family was engaged in a bitter winter's trek from Kentucky to Little Pigeon Creek in Indiana.

Lincoln's mother died when he was nine, but his father married again soon and his stepmother loved him and instilled in him an unfailing sense of justice. Lincoln heard about slaves and slavery, and he heard his elders talk about the Missouri Compromise of 1820–21—a series of compromises that, in the end, made Missouri a slave state and outlawed slavery, in what was to become Kansas-Nebraska Territory.

By his 17th birthday, Lincoln was sinewy, muscular and very strong. He was six feet four inches tall. After that, he grew no more in stature, but his capacity for growth in other ways was infinite. Some of his early statements about Africans and black Americans are offensive to us now but, by 1865, he had embraced black people as his equals and his brothers and sisters. In turn, black people were to move toward him and, at last, grow to love him. In 1865, Frederick Douglass—the greatest of black abolition-ists—who had often criticized Lincoln for his caution, was invited to the White House, following the inauguration ceremonies. There, Lincoln greeted Douglass cordially, then asked what he had thought of his inaugural address. Douglass answered, "Mr. Lincoln, that was a sacred effort." After Lincoln's death, Douglass, who had earlier referred to Lincoln as a white man's president, said, ". . . infinite wisdom has seldom sent any man into the world better fitted for his mission than Abraham Lincoln."

When he was 18, Lincoln's sister died. A year later, with a friend named Allen Gentry, who was close to Lincoln's age, Lincoln made a 1,200 mile journey down the Mississippi River to New Orleans on a flatboat, carrying a load of produce.

New Orleans, on a bend in the lower Mississippi, was a city that was known for its charm and wickedness. It was a hotbed of piracy, prostitution and slavery. On the streets leading northwest from the steamy waterfront, there were showrooms where slaves were on display. In New Orleans marketplaces, slaves were sold in the same manner as were animals, bales of cotton, casks of rum.

Several stories about Lincoln's first brush with slavery are repeated frequently, but most are, at best, half truths. Certainly, in New Orleans, Lincoln saw slaves in chains and slaves being sold, and he was struck, as if by lightning, by the cruelty of the institution. As Harriet Beecher Stowe was soon to demonstrate in *Uncle Tom's Cabin,* one of the most tragic aspects of the sale of human flesh was the splitting up of families. On auction blocks, wives and husbands lost their children, lost each other and their cousins, aunts and uncles, never to find them again. In slave markets, beautiful young women were stripped, prodded, sold to the owners of New Orleans pleasure domes or to lecherous plantation owners.

As Lincoln came of age, his family moved again, this time to a farm in Illinois, near Decatur. First he was a storekeeper, then a surveyor. In Lincoln's day, ambitious young men studied law and went into politics. As Lincoln taught himself the law and began to practice, Garrison's countrymen were beginning to respond to his insistence that they pay attention to the immorality of slavery. Centered in the Northeast, fired by Garrison and like-minded men and women, outrage over slavery flared and was soon to become a political inferno. Aristocratic Southerners, whose way of life depended on the continuance of slavery, looked for ways to protect it. Many Northerners believed that slavery couldn't be abolished altogether but must somehow be contained. Energetic young Americans were going west, pushing back and killing off the native population, clearing land, tilling soil. If something wasn't done to stop its spread, slavery would accompany or follow after settlement and, as more slave states joined the Union, slavery would overwhelm the federal government.

In 1834, Lincoln was elected to the Illinois House of Representatives. He was reelected three times, serving until 1842. In his 1836 campaign, he spoke not only against compromise over slavery but declared that women ought to have the right to vote—a right they had so far been denied.

In 1842, after a stormy courtship, Lincoln married Mary Todd. He served a term in the U.S. House of Representatives from 1847 to 1849. There, he opposed his country's war with Mexico—which was no more than a grab for a neighbor's territory—and proposed that slavery be abolished in the District of Columbia. Because of his firm stand on the war with Mexico, he was thought to be unpatriotic and, as a consequence, he retired from politics until 1854, when he became an eloquent opponent of the spread of slavery.

Six years before his first presidential campaign, Lincoln had expressed his view of slavery, which he saw as a moral evil and national disgrace.

I hate it because of the monstrous injustice of slavery itself. I hate it because it . . . enables the enemies of free institutions with plausibility to taunt us as hypocrites, causes the real friends of freedom to doubt our sincerity, and especially because it forces so many good men among ourselves into an open war with the very fundamental principles of civil liberty, criticizing the Declaration of Independence, and insisting that there is no right principle of action but self-interest.

It has been said that when the delegates from 12 states met in Philadelphia in 1787 and began to frame the Constitution, slavery was a sleeping serpent, coiled underneath the table. There were those who argued over its morality but, in the end, the signers of the Constitution had pretended that the serpent wasn't there. Lincoln understood this well and longed to strike a blow against the institution, but he was painfully aware of all the pieces in the puzzle he must try to solve, if he became president of the United States.

Compromises over slavery had been toyed with ever since 1820. None had worked. Congress, which was at times equally divided, was and remained a battleground for a complicated power struggle over the admission to the Union of free states and slave states. The 1850 Compromise, which included the second fugitive slave act—providing for the return of runaways to their masters—gave rise to violent opposition. In Boston, Thomas Wenworth Higginson, who was later to command a regiment of black soldiers, failed in an attempt to free Anthony Burns, an escaped slave from Virginia who was captured under a provision of the act.

Finally, passage of the Kansas-Nebraska Act, of 1854, which swept away the Missouri Compromise, of 1820–21—including its provision outlawing slavery in the Kansas-Nebraska Territory—infuriated antislavery legislators. The act, shepherded through Congress by Lincoln's perennial opponent Stephen Douglas, left decisions about slavery to the settlers themselves, allowing public territories to become slave states. In promoting passage of this act, Douglas made what most historians think of as a blunder. The provisions of the act were explosive, promoting sectional disputes and, at last, driving North and South so far apart that a rift became a certainty.

Passage of the act led directly to formation of the Republican Party, whose main purpose was to prevent the spread of slavery into western territories. The great reservoir of Southern bitterness erupted violently in 1856 when leading abolitionist Senator Charles Sumner suffered a vicious beating by South Carolina Congressman Preston Brooks, in which Sumner's head was bloodied and he sank unconscious to the floor of the Senate chamber.

Lincoln saw that war was coming, and he believed that if the South won the war, slavery would run rampant in America and would, in time, destroy democracy. He believed that the North must win the coming war and, even as he ran for office, he used every means at his command to keep as many states and territories as he could on the side of the Union and persuade foreign powers—especially Britain—not to give aid and comfort to the South.

In the spring of 1860, the Democratic Party, which, at that time, was clearly more conservative than the Republican Party, was fragmented. That summer, Stephen Douglas—who had debated Lincoln off and on from 1839 to 1858—and two other candidates, John C. Breckenridge and John Bell, each formed parties of their own and thus began a four-way race, in which Lincoln—the Republican nominee—seemed to have the upper hand, though he wasn't sure of winning. The Republicans reaffirmed their unity and reiterated their resolve to win New York State with its 35 electoral votes, or risk having the election thrown into Congress, where the Democrats might have a chance of winning.

William Lowndes Yancey, a portly, charming Southern politician, traveled north to New York to speak against the candidate he most feared. Yancey represented the secessionists—those who favored slavery and believed that the South must separate from the Union to preserve its way of life. Lincoln, on the other hand, had gone on record as believing that no nation could, ". . . endure permanently half slave and half free." However, in his effort to preserve the Union, he was willing to let slavery stand where it existed, at least until another compromise could be worked out. This was not enough for Yancey, who was born in Georgia and spoke for his fellow Southerners who believed that to stop the spread of slavery was tantamount to declaring it illegal everywhere.

When Yancey rose to speak, there was something in his manner that drew the attention of his audience. At first, he spoke in a soft voice but what he said was instructive. He scorned the abolitionists. He was witty and he often drew applause. He praised the Constitution. Then he spoke of slavery. "So, gentlemen, this institution is necessary to your prosperity as well as ours. It is an institution, too, that doesn't harm you, for we don't let our niggers run about to injure anybody."

On November 4, Lincoln won the election and, on March 4, 1861, was sworn in as the country's 16th president. As he took office, war seemed unavoidable. The breakdown of compromise over slavery had eroded any chance of unity. The North boasted a much larger population than the South. Its industries were flourishing. On the other hand, the South depended heavily on the health of its plantations, which were worked by its four million slaves. At this stage, many Northerners were reluctant to begin a war while wealthy and aristocratic Southeners were eager to take up their swords and fight for their way of life.

On December 20, South Carolina passed an ordinance of secession. Power in the South was now in the hands of a radical minority. South Carolina was already bent on war and secession fever spread like wildfire. During the next six weeks, Mississippi, Florida, Alabama, Georgia, Louisiana and Texas left the Union. Delegates from these states met, drew up a constitution and formed their own government.

As the Confederacy laid claim to all the forts and batteries in Confederate territory, including Fort Sumter, Shaw's life began to take a definite direction. On April 5, he wrote to his sister Susie, who was still in Cambridge,

> We have exciting news today from the South. It is now almost certain that Mr. Lincoln is going to re-enforce the United States forts, and in that case the Southerners will almost surely resist. All the vessels of the Navy are being got ready for sea, and several sail from here today.

Major Robert Anderson, in command of Fort Sumter, was born in Kentucky and had lived in Virginia but was nonetheless a Unionist. Following Lincoln's notice that a naval expedition would be sent to provision the beleagured island bastion, Confederate General P. G. T. Beauregard demanded Anderson's surrender.

Anderson refused and, on April 12, the Confederates opened fire on the fort and war began.

After that, things moved fast for Shaw and for his nation. Shaw, who had once favored a division of the country, was now a Unionist who wouldn't hear of compromise. He wrote, "As for making concessions, it is only patching up the affair for a year or two, when it would break out worse than ever." Whatever he had thought before, Shaw now saw the need for force.

Confederate soldiers had begun to gather in Virginia, just south of Washington, and when Lincoln called for volunteers to defend the capital, Shaw was among the first to go. He joined the Seventh New York National Guard, serving first as a private. The regiment—which was and still is referred to simply as the Seventh regiment—was made up of rich, sometimes patrician, often arrogant New Yorkers. Shaw, who had sometimes fretted over his lack of height, had never questioned his position as the son of American aristocrats and so was altogether comfortable as a private in the Seventh.

His departure for the capital was unexpected, and his parents were vacationing in Cuba. On May 18, he wrote his father, "We go off tomorrow afternoon, and hope to be in Washington the following day." He confessed, "I can't help crying a little when I think of mother and you and the girls. God bless you all."

The departure of the Seventh was heralded and celebrated all the way down Broadway, from the Tompkins Market Armory to Cortlandt Street, where it turned west to make the short march to the ferry that would take them to the New Jersey Railroad Depot. One of Shaw's comrades-in-arms wrote,

> It was worth a life, that march. Only one who passed, as we did, through that tempest of cheers, two miles long, can know the terrible enthusiasm of the occasion. I could hardly hear the rattle of our own gun carriages, and only twice the music of our band came to me, muffled and quelled by the uproar.

At the depot, an enormous throng had gathered on the galleries and platforms. The stars and stripes and brightly colored banners hung below the arching girders of the roof. Sweethearts said goodbye to loved ones, giving them small bouquets tied with ribbons saying MAY PEACE BRING YOU

Shaw in New York's Seventh Regiment. (Massachusetts Historical Society)

BACK TO ME. The men were showered with things they might want or would need—hampers of sandwiches, fruit baskets, flasks of liquor.

Bonfires lined the right of way as the men in the train were carried south. As the regiment arrived in Philadelphia, they were greeted wildly once again. A few days earlier, the passage of the Sixth Massachusetts through Baltimore—a Secessionist stronghold—had set off a full-scale riot in which 36 members of the regiment had been wounded and four killed and a number of civilians wounded. In order to avoid the risk of more bloodshed, the Seventh was put aboard the steamer *Boston,* which made its way south on the Delaware River and Delaware Bay, into the Atlantic Ocean. While Shaw was sleeping, the steamer entered Chesapeake Bay and, as the mists of morning thinned, docked at Annapolis, where they spent the night; in the early morning hours, they marched to a whistle stop on the railroad line to Washington.

The Seventh rolled into Washington at noon. A reporter for the New York *Tribune* wrote of the Seventh's march down Pennsylvania Avenue, "When in place of the drums and fifes, the full band struck up, the whole city danced with delight." Well it might. The enemy was at its gates and the arrival of more troops from the North was reassuring.

Shaw found the city almost like a frontier town. Its streets were muddy and the White House seemed a kind of country mansion. Although George Washington had laid its corner- stone in 1793, the capitol was incomplete. Burned by the British in the War of 1812, it had been rebuilt and expanded, but its dome had not been finished. Shaw's company was quartered in the House of Representatives where Shaw slept on his bedroll in an aisle. He wrote happily, "Hope to see Old Abe soon."

The next day dawned bright and clear. The president was on hand when the men of the Seventh took an oath to serve the federal government for 30 days. Lincoln stood between his two younger sons—Tad and Willie—holding hands with both of them. Shaw wrote,

> Old Abe stood out in front of us, looking as pleasant and kind as possible, and, when we presented arms, took off his hat in the most awkward way, putting it on again with his hand on the back of the rim, country fashion. A boy came up with a pail of water for us, and the President took a great swig from it as it passed. I couldn't help thinking of the immense responsibility he has on his shoulders, as he stood there laughing and talking.

Shaw swept the floor of the House of Representatives, did other menial chores and had time to poke about the city. On April 30, with Rufus King, a soldier in his company, Shaw paid a call on Lincoln. He remembered,

> After waiting a few minutes in an antechamber, we were shown into into a room where Mr. Lincoln was sitting at a desk perfectly covered with papers of every description. He got up and shook hands with us both in the most cordial way, asked us to be seated, and seemed quite glad to have us come. It is really too bad to call him one of the ugliest men in the country, for I have seldom seen a pleasanter or more kind-hearted looking one and he has certainly a very striking face. It is easy to see why he is so popular with all who come into contact with him. His voice is very pleasant. . . . He gives you the impression, too, of being a gentleman.

Shaw saw no action with the Seventh. As his enlistment ran its course, he applied for a commission in the Second Massachusetts, which was under the command of Colonel George H. Gordon.

Shaw left the Seventh, was commissioned May 18, and went into camp in West Roxbury, close to where he had lived as a boy. He liked Gordon—a handsome West Point graduate with deep-set eyes. Shaw had many friends in the Second, first among them his cousin Henry Russell.

The camp consisted of several hundred canvas tents covering a grassy hill. Gordon was a hard taskmaster and here, perhaps for the first time, Shaw became altogether serious about his work. He liked being an officer. On his first day in camp, he wrote to his mother, who was fussing constantly over his health and safety, "There is a great difference between the life of a private and that of an officer, I find. We have cots to sleep on, much better fare, and servants in abundance among the men." Later, in the field, Shaw was to lose a number of his comrades in combat, and he would have to do without the luxuries he enjoyed in West Roxbury.

Only July 8, the regiment went by rail, then by steamer, in moonlight, to New York and on by rail to Williamsport, Maryland, where it forded the Potomac, marching into what was soon to become West Virginia. There, the Second joined the command of General Robert Patterson whose job it was to engage a Confederate force under General Thomas Jackson—later to be called Stonewall Jackson—in the Shenandoah Valley, which ran north and south between the Blue Ridge and the Allegheny Mountains. The valley, it was thought, would be a fine protected route for invasion of the North but, at that time, Jackson was engaging in diversionary tactics and Patterson and his successor, General Nathaniel Banks, were to be repeatedly deceived by him.

Shaw loved the Shenandoah Valley, marvelled at the glories of the countryside, delighted in the golden fields and peach and apple orchards and the mountains in the distance. The young man who had witnessed the beauty of Swiss mountains wrote, "I never saw anything so beautiful."

As war began, the North seemed stronger than the South. It had twice the manpower and its many factories could produce 30 times as much as could be manufactured in the South, but the South had a proud military heritage and a distinguished president—Jefferson Davis, a Southern planter. Davis had graduated from West Point, had served with distinction in the army and had been a U.S. Senator from Mississippi, before being sworn in—on February 18, 1862—as president of the Confederacy.

Lincoln had none of Davis's credentials, but he was intelligent and energetic, a wise man who possessed great breadth of vision and a purity of spirit. These were qualities that were to assert themselves repeatedly and make him someone destined to be honored through the ages. However, as he took command, his inexperience, together with what at first was a shortage of good fighting generals—men who could match the skill, the courage and the dash of Southerners—disappointed Union hopes for an early victory and, several times, were to imperil Washington itself.

The most capable of Lincoln's generals was Winfield Scott, whose career dated back to the War of 1812 and who had long been a hero to his countrymen. Scott was a Virginian but was a loyal Unionist. He had lost none of his acuity but was growing old and was in a weakened physical condition. His heir-apparent was 34-year-old George McClellan who, in June and July of 1861, had chased Confederate forces out of the Virginia mountains. McClellan was a good organizer and extremely popular with his men, but he possessed a fatal flaw that would soon reveal itself.

With Scott, McClellan and several other of his generals, Lincoln had fashioned a grand strategy called the Anaconda Plan, which involved a blockade of Southern ports on the Atlantic and Gulf coasts and eventual control of the Mississippi River. The blockade, designed to keep foreign powers—mostly England—from trading arms and ammunition for the products of the South, was to be only partially successful. The Union had a small and efficient navy, but more than 3,000 miles of coastline lay between New Orleans and the Chesapeake, and not all of it could be policed.

During the first year of war, as Confederate forces menaced Washington, the Anaconda Plan gave Lincoln little comfort. McClellan's token victories were followed by a long series of disasters in the East. The first of these occurred on July 21, when Union forces, moving south hoping to defeat General Beauregard at Manassas Junction near Bull Run Creek, were repulsed when Beauregard was joined by Jackson who had unexpectedly moved east across the mountains. The retreat became a rout as young and frightened volunteers fled north on country roads that were jammed with civilians—men and women in their finest clothes who had come down from Washington with picnic baskets to sit on a nearby hill and watch what they were sure would be an easy Union victory. These were people who had thought of war as a series of isolated battles, fought almost as a game and not involving the civilian population. This war, of course, was soon to threaten and engage large numbers of civilians.

Bull Run was the first important battle of the Civil War, and the defeat frightened many Northerners. Shaw and his friends took a sanguine view of the defeat, which had been humiliating but not in any way decisive. Shaw wrote his father that he was, ". . . astonished at your feeling so badly about the 'Bull Run' battle." Shaw found the news unwelcome ". . . but thought it would do our troops good, as they had begun to think the Southerners would run every time they were attacked."

After the defeat at Bull Run, Lincoln, who didn't like McClellan much but understood the value of his popularity, asked him to organize the army that defended Washington.

At that stage, Lincoln thought that there was something to be said for polished buttons and belt buckles and close-order drill.

Meanwhile, Nathaniel Banks replaced Patterson as Shaw's corps commander and the Second moved from point to point in the Shenandoah Valley, trying to keep track of Jackson, who had come west from Manassas. In long lulls between tentative engagements, Shaw found time for reading and reflection. His growing abolitionist convictions, together with his friendship with like-minded fellow officers, prompted him to write an important letter to Sidney Howard Gay, who was by then on the staff of the New York *Tribune.* "Isn't it extraordinary that the Government won't make use of the instrument that would finish the war sooner than anything else,—viz. the slaves?" He went on, "What a lick it would be to them [the Secessionists], to call on all the blacks in the country to come and enlist in our army! They would probably make a fine army after a little drill, and could certainly be kept under better discipline than our independent Yankees."

The officer who most influenced Shaw in this regard was Major Morris Copeland—a sturdy bearded man with a high forehead, bright eyes and a face that suggested keen intelligence. Copeland was described by Shaw as a hard worker and a most efficient officer. Copeland campaigned tirelessly for black participation in a war that he hoped would sweep the country free of slavery. He was soon to talk to Banks about the matter. Banks was destined to be sent to New Orleans where, as commander of the Department of the Gulf, he would remember Copeland's arguments and employ black soldiers.

Shaw was eager to play an active part in a war that was going very badly for the Union. In fact, there was talk in the hotels and saloons of Washington about England making war against the North, unless the North chalked up an important victory in the East. In his *History of the English Speaking Peoples,* Winston S. Churchill wrote about European attitudes toward the war following a year of conflict. "So far, the American Civil War had appeared to Europe as a desultory brawl of mobs and partisans which might at any time be closed by politics and parley." France sympathized with the Confederacy and would have given it diplomatic recognition had England led the way. England's Queen Victoria was in favor of neutrality but her nation was divided. The blockade of Southern ports by Union

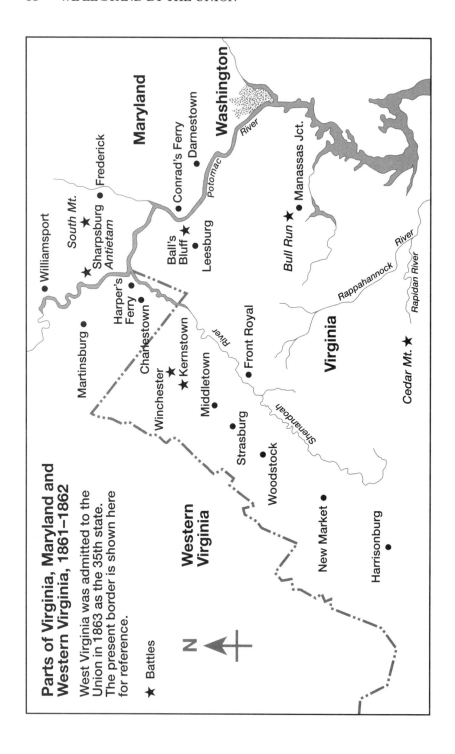

Parts of Virginia, Maryland and Western Virginia, 1861–1862

West Virginia was admitted to the Union in 1863 as the 35th state. The present border is shown here for reference.

★ Battles

ships had produced a cotton famine that was hurting British industry and the arrest by a Union officer of two Confederate agents found on a British blockade runner raised the anger of the British populace. Lincoln apologized for the action, saying wisely, "One war at a time." He set the two men free, but the episode was not forgotten. Lincoln waited for a time when he could issue an emancipation proclamation, transforming the Civil War into a clear moral conflict in which he believed England would come down on the right side.

On Christmas day 1861, referring to the possibility of war with England, Shaw wrote, "War isn't declared yet, but doesn't it look very much like it to everyone at home?"

The Second went into winter quarters near Darnestown, Maryland, and, as spring touched the countryside, Shaw found himself in camp in Charles Town, Virginia, surrounded by gentle hills and fertile farms. Charles Town evoked sharp images of a story Shaw knew well. Here, less than three years earlier, the already legendary John Brown had been tried, convicted and hung—in a lot between McCurdy Street and Beckwith Alley. After the execution, an officer who was one of 1,500 soldiers who had taken part in the proceeding, called out, "So perisheth all such enemies of Virginia, all such enemies of the Union, all such foes of the human race!"

A spare man, Brown had penetrating eyes and a nose like a hawk's bill. He was at once both stern and gentle. Married twice, he fathered 20 children. Not only his first wife but many of his children died before him. Born in Connecticut, having farmed in New York State, he had gone to the Kansas Territory to live near the Ossawatomie River, in a colony of free-state settlers—those who opposed the spread of slavery into what they hoped would soon become a free state. There, in response to the killing of five free-state settlers by Border Ruffians—men from Missouri who favored slavery and harassed and sometimes killed those opposed to slavery—he led six men, including four of his sons, in the butchery of five pro-slavery settlers.

Brown had long since worked out a strategy for setting off a chain of slave revolts, which he believed would become a widespread revolution. In 1848, he invited Frederick Douglass to his home and outlined his plan for freeing the slaves. He saw the Appalachian Mountain Range, which reached from Maine to the

Alabama border, as a shaft that might be driven through the heart of slavery. He believed that he could start with a small band of men and establish mountain fortresses, from which he could reach out and recruit willing fugitive slaves who would become the nucleus of a vast liberating army, which would grow as it moved south. When this force was strong enough, perhaps numbering 100 men who had been brave enough to risk their lives for their freedom, it would attract many thousands to its ranks, sparking dozens of revolts. Douglass argued that the initial force would attract much attention and would in time be pinned down in its mountain fortress and destroyed. At this stage of his career, Douglass believed that slaveholders might be reasoned with. Brown knew better. He thought that his plan would work and he clung tenaciously to it.

Accordingly, more than 10 years later, on October 16, 1859, with 21 men, two of whom were his sons and five of whom were black, he began his campaign by capturing the U.S. arsenal at Harper's Ferry, Virginia. There, he was unexpectedly boxed in by local militiamen and, in the morning, was attacked by a small force of U.S. Marines, under Colonel Robert E. Lee. In the ensuing battle, Brown was forced to surrender. The raid cost the lives of 16 of Brown's men killed outright, attempting to escape or later executed by the State of Virginia. Some were taken prisoner. Others made good their escape. Some of those who escaped were recaptured. Others fled to Canada. One innocent onlooker was shot in the back and killed and of those who opposed Brown, four were killed.

Brown himself was wounded and, as he lay in pain, was asked by one of his captors, "On what principle do you justify your acts?" Brown replied,

> Upon the Golden Rule. I pity the poor in bondage that have none to help them; that is why I am here; not to gratify any personal animosity, revenge or vindictive spirit. It is my sympathy with the oppressed and wronged, that are as good as you and as precious in the sight of God. . . . You may dispose of me easily but this question is still to be settled—this Negro question—the end of that is still not yet.

Disapproving as nonviolent abolitionists were of Brown's bloody methods, most of them had come to realize that no fiery

From left to right: James Savage, Shaw, Morris Copeland, Henry Sturgis Russell. This photograph was taken in 1862, when these men were serving in the Massachusetts Second. Savage died of wounds sustained at Cedar Mountain. Shaw had known his cousin Henry Russell since childhood. They had entered Harvard in the same class and were devoted to each other. Morris Copeland advocated the enlistment of black soldiers. (From the collection of the author)

speech, no biting editorial would, in itself, free the several million slaves held in bondage in America's southland. Brown became their hero. Theodore Parker, who had been the Shaw's friend and minister, in West Roxbury, and had gone to live in Italy, declared John Brown a saint. He wrote, "The road to Heaven is as short from the gallows as from a throne."

The reaction of Shaw's mother's friend Lydia Maria Child, who wrote to Brown as he awaited execution, was typical of the kind of sentiment expressed by nonviolent abolitionists. "I admire your courage, moral and physical, I reverence you for the humanity which tempered your zeal, I sympathize with your cruel bereavements, your sufferings, and your wrongs. In brief, I love and bless you."

Philosopher Ralph Waldo Emerson said that Brown had, ". . . made the gallows as glorious as the cross."

Shaw walked through the dusty streets of Charles Town, passing shops and graceful houses, many of them built in the century before. He stopped at the courthouse, on the northeast corner of Washington and George Streets. Built in 1836 to replace a smaller structure, the red brick Georgian building was impressive. Set on a high stone foundation, it was fronted by a narrow portico, supported by four Doric columns and topped by a clock tower.

Most of the county records had been removed to Lexington, Virginia, for safekeeping but, when Shaw gained entrance to the abandoned office of Andrew Hunter—prosecuting attorney at Brown's trial—he found drawers full of fascinating papers. He saw many documents that related to Brown's trial. He read transcripts of the testimony and confessions of some members of Brown's company. He found, ". . . letters from people in all parts of the country, some interceding for Brown, and some hoping and praying that he would be executed without delay." He studied notes that Brown had written, ". . . on as many as a hundred scraps of paper covered with the finest possible writing, which appear to be the notes for sermons." He commented, "They are hard to read when deciphered, unintelligible in great measure as they seem to be the revelation of dreams, and all sorts of strange fancies."

Shaw's friend Jim Savage, whose square jaw and long moustache made him an impressive looking officer, went with Shaw, Morris Copeland and Harry Russell to the jail where Brown had been confined. Copeland wrote about the visit, "The old cot was there on which he [Brown] lay during his imprisonment." The four men sat down on the cot and, then and there, worked out a plan, later approved by their superiors, under which slaves would be recognized as free as they entered Union lines. Copeland noted optimistically, "Thus, within three years, John Brown's work was completed on the very spot where he died to testify his belief in the principles of human equality and justice."

Shaw's face-to-face encounter with this evidence of Brown's humanity, of his work and of his martyrdom, had a profound effect on him. With his enlistment in the Second, he had become a dedicated soldier. Now, Brown's story, in a sense, became his own, and he saw that the war in which he was now engaged must soon become a war of liberation.

In the spring of 1862, for the first time, Shaw thought of serving as an officer in a black regiment. On May 19, he wrote his father,

> You will be surprised to see that I am in Washington. I came down with Major Copeland to see if I could assist him at all, in a plan he has made for getting up a black regiment. He says, very justly, that it would be much wiser to enlist men in the North, who have had the courage to run away, and have already suffered for their freedom, than to take them all from contrabands at Port Royal and other places.

4
TURNING POINT
1862

On the morning of September 16, 1862 Shaw, in the Massachusetts Second, having made a two-day march from Frederick, Maryland, halted near Antietam Creek, two miles north of Sharpsburg.

This was hilly country, crisscrossed by narrow roads and winding lanes, graced by rolling pasturelands and fields of wheat and tasseled corn. The white frame houses were as plain as the good people who lived in them—farmers who cared little for the war. Here, Shaw would take part in his first major battle, a contest that was to mark a turning point in his life and in the history of America.

On this fateful day, on which Union and Confederate armies faced each other across Antietam Creek, few European diplomats believed that the North could win the war. So far, Charles Francis Adams—Lincoln's ambassador to Britain—had been successful in forestalling Britain's recognition of the Confederacy, but there was an increasing possibility that Britain, and then France, would abandon their neutrality. Lately, it had seemed that Lincoln's will was the only force that had kept he Union from disintegrating altogether. Even in Lincoln's darkest hour, he expressed his determination to keep fighting. "I expect to maintain this contest until successful, or till I die."

Spring and summer had brought widespread military action in the East, which had cost many lives and had brought no resolution. In order to follow Shaw and to comprehend the depth of the crisis of the Union, we need to understand the military situation, especially in the East, where Shaw had been serving in an army that was constantly outmaneuvered and outfought, and in which morale was sinking fast.

In the spring of 1862, fighting was in progress mostly on or near the Mississippi River and in Virginia. As part of the execution of the Anaconda Plan, New Orleans had recently been captured by Admiral David Farragut and General Benjamin Butler. Confederate strongholds on the Mississippi had been attacked and captured by aggressive Northern generals. General Ulysses S. Grant, who was fighting for the Union in the West, was emerging as a leader to be reckoned with.

Lincoln was reassured by successes in the West, but Washington and Richmond—the respective capitals of the warring nations—were both in the East and were separated by less than 100 miles as the crow flies. The Potomac—snaking down from Williamsport, running past Harper's Ferry and Ball's Bluff and broadening as it was fed by the waters of the Anacosta—gave considerable protection to the capital in Washington. Batteries lined the shores of the Potomac and its bridges were patrolled. Washington was easier to defend than Richmond, but it had been threatened more often.

The clever and aggressive Jackson, moving back and forth between the Shenandoah Valley and the northern reaches of Virginia, had continued to harass Shaw's corps commander General Banks. While Banks parried Jackson's thrusts, often suffering humiliation, McClellan moved on the Confederate capital. He could have gone overland, across the Virginia countryside, but a direct approach to Richmond would have forced him to engage his enemy, something he was loathe to do. He chose instead to take 200,000 men down the broad Potomac, into the Chesapeake, to the long peninsula between the York and James rivers, in what came to be known as the Peninsula or Peninsular Campaign. As he prepared to lay siege to Confederate lines near the end of the peninsula, his enemy withdrew to a point nine miles from Richmond, after scuttling the ironclad ship *Merrimack*—renamed the *Virginia*—which on March 9 had engaged in an indecisive duel with the ironclad *Monitor*.

On May 16, having gained control of both rivers, McClellan established his headquarters at White House Landing, 20 miles east of Richmond, where he faced an army half the size of his but failed to press his advantage. In the Seven Days

Battle, he was stopped by Robert E. Lee, who by then was in command of the Army of Northern Virginia. In fact, on August 13, as McClellan started his retreat, he could have overwhelmed the Confederate capital and brought an early end to war.

Meanwhile, in the Shenandoah Valley, Shaw grew bored with inaction. On April 5, he wrote to his sister Nellie, "We are doing nothing now, as as has been our custom for eight months." At last, on May 25, several weeks after he had traveled north for a visit with his family, he found himself involved in a retreat from a regiment of Jackson's soldiers in the streets of Winchester, where he was shot at, not only by Confederate riflemen, but by civilians firing from the doorways and the windows of their houses. Here Shaw's life was saved by his gold watch. "The ball would undoubtedly have entered my stomach, and as it was bruised my hip a great deal."

Following his brush with death, remembering his visit with his family, he wrote touchingly to his father, "So when I felt the blow on my side & found my watch had stopped the ball, the first thing I thought of was how you all would have felt if I had been left on that infernal pavement & it seemed as if I could see you all standing on the piazza just before I came away."

After the encounter at Winchester, Shaw was praised for his coolness under fire and, when Colonel Gordon was promoted to the rank of major general, he asked Shaw to become his adjutant. Shaw accepted and became a captain.

In late June, General John A. Pope, who had captured Island Number Ten—in a bend of the Mississippi River at New Madrid, Missouri—came east hoping to achieve success in a theater where there had been only failures. Pope took command of the newly formed Army of Virginia, which consisted of the Union forces in the Shenandoah Valley, under Banks, and others that were strung along the Rappahannock. Shaw saw Pope and was not impressed with him. "He looks just what we have always thought he was—a great *blow-hard*."

Shaw was right about Pope but, despite his many disappointments and his lack of confidence in his commander, he remained an optimist. "There is no doubt that good will ultimately come of this war; that slavery will disappear, and the country eventually be united; but I begin to doubt that we shall accomplish it by force of arms."

In Virginia, on August 9, Banks was attacked again by Jackson at a hill named Cedar Mountain, near Culpeper. In the ensuing battle, Union forces were defeated. While the battle was in progress, Shaw saw his cousin Henry Russell. Afterward, Shaw wrote, "I was about opposite to his company and a few paces in the rear and he called out, 'Hullo Bob!' and came to where I was. We talked a few minutes together about what was going on, and then he went back to his place and stood, pulling his moustache and looking over the field, the bullets whistling thick around him. He was perfectly quiet but he looked pretty fierce."

Russell and Savage were taken prisoner that day. Later, Russell—held at Libby Prison in Richmond—was exchanged. He rose to the rank of colonel and was wounded but survived the war. Savage subsequently died of wounds sustained at Cedar Mountain.

Late that afternoon, Shaw, unaware of what had happened to his cousin or to Savage, toured the battlefield and found the bodies of five other soldiers he had known. He was especially touched by the sight of Richard Carey who, with his wife, had lived in the South before the war but was a Unionist. He wrote of Carey, "He was lying on his back with his head on a piece of wood. He looked calm and peaceful as if he were merely sleeping; his face was beautiful, and I could have looked at it a long while." Shaw wrote of the dead, "Oh! it is hard to believe that we will never see them again."

After Cedar Mountain, Shaw spent a night and a morning resting in a wood near Culpeper, before beginning what Pope hoped would be an unimpeded march northwest toward Washington. Shaw wrote about the hardships he had suffered on the march. "We have been drenched with rain & scorched with sun—have slept much of the time on the ground without blankets & have lived principally on green apples & corn. Sometimes really almost starving."

As it happened, Pope wasn't destined to escape without engaging in the second Battle of Bull Run. After Cedar Mountain, Jackson split his army into three separate parts, surreptitiously moving those three parts toward a rendezvous with Lee, who was marching north from Richmond.

Though an observation balloon had been used by McClellan during his timid moves in the Peninsula Campaign, there was of course no effective aerial reconnaissance during the Civil War and Jackson's moves so baffled Pope that, when Pope finally found him on a wooded ridge northwest of the first Bull Run battlefield, he thought he was retreating. Pope then blundered into battle, lacking a coherent plan and, though at first he commanded a much stronger force than Jackson's, Jackson held his ground long enough to be reenforced by Lee. In the end, Pope's bluster proved to be as damaging as McClellan's lack of courage, and the two Southern generals—who had always worked efficiently together—handed Pope a shattering defeat.

Shaw was not involved directly in the humiliating battle. Pope had instructed Banks to guard his supply routes—bridges, wagon roads and railroad lines—while the battle was in progress. The next day, Shaw wrote, "Yesterday we were said to have been out off from the main army. We burnt a large train of cars. . . . " At last, he expressed discouragement. "This campaign began about the 1st of March. Now it is September & we are just where we started from. Just think of the Rebel Army being at Manassas again." He went on, "We shall never do much until we get a very different army from what we have now. . . . There is a total want of discipline & system throughout. In every battle a part of the men skulk & after a day's march the roads are lined with stragglers." Shaw's understanding of the need for discipline was to become apparent as he trained the Fifty Fourth.

Pope's defeat in the second Battle of Bull Run led to an event that, as much as any other, demonstrated the depth of the military crisis Lincoln faced and why it was that he kept on employing McClellan, in one way or another, even after the unsatisfactory outcome of the Peninsula Campaign.

Following the second Battle of Bull Run, when some of McClellan's soldiers—in fresh uniforms and polished boots— came down from Washington, supposedly to save the day, they saw Pope's exhausted and defeated men and jeered at them. There was something in McClellan that evoked nothing short of adoration and it seemed that his soldiers had believed that a defeat for Pope meant triumph for their hero. Lincoln must by then have understood the weakness of McClellan, but he knew that if he dismissed him he might face a mutiny in the army that defended Washington.

After its defeat at Bull Run, Pope's army—scattered and relentlessly pursued by an aggressive enemy—started a retreat toward Washington, stopped once, engaging its pursuers in a rearguard action in a crashing thunderstorm, then moved on to the banks of the Potomac, close to Washington.

Lee's victory at Bull Run encouraged him to cross the Potomac in its shallow upper reaches and go north, a move that was to lead to the Battle of Antietam.

Banks's corps now left Pope and moved to join McClellan, whose main body was in Washington. It crossed the Potomac and made camp just outside the capital, where it spent four days, while Union scouts made sure that Lee's move was not a feint. The corps then joined McClellan whose vast army had begun to move northwest, in great parallel advances, to meet Lee, in Frederick, Maryland.

Though Lee had told Confederate President Jefferson Davis—who favored a defensive war—that his intention was to keep McClellan busy so he wouldn't launch a fresh attack on Richmond, he was secretly ambitious. In fact, he hoped to march all the way to Harrisburg, Pennsylvania, and destroy the railroad bridge across the Susquehanna River, thus severing the main line to the West. He told one of his commanders, "After that I can turn my attention to Philadelphia, Baltimore or Washington, as may seem best for our interests."

His listener expressed astonishment at the audacity of Lee's plan, but Lee, in his quiet voice, went on to talk about McClellan's character. "He is an able general but a very cautious one." In fact, Lee believed that, by the time McClellan moved, he could be in Harrisburg. So bold was Lee that he told Jackson to stop off and capture the Union garrison at Harper's Ferry—numbering 10,000 men. This would divide and weaken Lee's army but would keep the Shenandoah Valley free of Union troops, so that it could serve as a supply route and a highway for retreat.

As was his habit, Jackson moved as fast as possible. After taking Harper's Ferry, he left it lightly garrisoned and moved north to join Lee. His men marched in tattered shoes and ragged uniforms. They had very little food but, having raided Harper's Ferry, were supplied with new rifles and a store of ammunition. Lee, in a weakened state without Jackson, chose not to fight at Frederick and withdrew across South Mountain to Sharpsburg, west of Antietam Creek, where he waited for Jackson and his troops.

Shaw marched through the town of Frederick, where people cheered wave after wave of Union soldiers. The bells in the church towers pealed incessantly. The stars and stripes were on display in front of all the shops and public buildings.

As McClellan's army moved west across the mountain, one of Shaw's fellow officers noted that McClellan hadn't lost his popularity. When the General—a small man on a fine horse—appeared on the National Road, ". . . caps flew in the air, and shouts and cheers rolled up as if from one man. . . . They believed in McClellan."

On September 16, Shaw and his company took up a position in a field, on the edge of a wood, a mile and a half north of Sharpsburg, ". . . and lay there all day." It was on that day that Banks was replaced by white-whiskered General Mansfield.

McClellan, whose reputation had been crippled by his failure to take Richmond, was being given every chance to prove that he could be aggressive. Not only was his army once again more than twice as large as Lee's but, two days earlier, he had had an extraordinary stroke of luck, which had given him a second chance to end the war. A copy of Special Order 191, containing Lee's battle plans, was given to him by one of his subordinates. This vital document, which had apparently been lost by a Confederate courier, had been found by Union soldiers in a large envelope, wrapped around three cigars. The order told of Lee's intention to engage in a complicated series of maneuvers, which included Jackson's Harper's Ferry operation. Had Mc-Clellan moved swiftly to attack Lee before Lee was reenforced by Jackson, he could have have destroyed Lee's army, but he hesitated once again, giving Jackson time to rejoin Lee.

Shaw wrote his father, giving him an account of his movements at the Battle of Antietam. On the night of September 16, he visited William Forbes—son of John Murray Forbes who, as a charter member of what came to be called the Black Committee, was to play an important part in the recruitment of Shaw's Fifty Fourth Massachusetts Regiment. "The Massachusetts Cavalry was very near us. I went over and spent the evening with them and had a long talk with Will Forbes about home and friends there. . . . We lay on a blanket by the fire, until nearly 10 o'clock, and then I left him, little realizing what the next day was to be, though a battle was expected." As he walked back to his regiment, Shaw wondered if he would ever see Forbes again.

As it happened, both of them survived a day that took more lives than any other single day in the war.

The Union lines had formed roughly north and south, facing west. They were made up of General Joseph Hooker's corps on the right—facing Dunker Church, a mile or so north of Sharpsburg—and Mansfield's corps just behind Hooker's men. General Edwin Sumner's corps was below Mansfield and Hooker, on their left, while General Ambrose Burnside's corps faced a bridge across Antietam Creek, southeast of town. Lee's army, facing this vast array of Union troops, was much weaker than McClellan's. Had he not been one of history's boldest generals, he would not have fought at Sharpsburg.

Following a day of inactivity, Shaw wrote, "At one in the morning of the 17th, we rested in a wheat-field. Our pickets were firing all night." At dawn, Shaw was awakened by the repeated thud of Hooker's cannon as he leveled a cornfield near Dunker Church. Shaw's company, now in Mansfield's corps, moved forward under heavy fire to join the fight at the church. Shaw wrote later, "I never felt before, the excitement which makes a man want to rush into the fight, but I did that day." Shaw's company was posted in an orchard near the church, which was bounded by a split rail fence. The Third Wisconsin, which was fighting close to the Massachusetts Second, lost 200 killed or wounded within minutes but was saved from annihilation by crossfire from Shaw's regiment. "It was the prettiest thing we have ever done and our loss was small."

As Shaw's company advanced across a field that had been held by Confederate riflemen, he found many fallen soldiers. ". . . such a mass of dead and wounded men, mostly Rebels, as were lying there, I never saw before; it was a terrible sight, and our men had to be very careful to avoid treading on them; many were mangled and torn to pieces by artillery, but most of them had been wounded by musketry fire."

Mansfield's corps moved forward through the cornfield, driving the enemy before it, until it finally lost momentum and paused in an open field close to the church. Shaw wrote of the wounded, "We halted right among them, and the men did everything they could for their comfort, giving them water from our canteens, and trying to place them in easy positions. There are so many old men and young boys among the Rebels, that it seems hardly possible that they can have come of their own accord to fight us, and it makes you pity them all the more, as they lie moaning on the field." Shaw went on, "The wounded Rebels were always as surprised and grateful as men could be at receiving attention from us, and many said that all they wanted was to get into our hospitals, and wished they had never fired a shot at us." One boy in his teens told Shaw's friend and fellow officer Charles Morse that, ". . . he had left North Carolina three weeks ago, and how his father and mother grieved at his going."

As Shaw and his men ministered to their fallen enemies, "Sumner's whole corps swept across, close by us, and advanced into a wood . . . It was a grand sight. . . . " Invincible as it looked, Sumner's corps was driven back. One Union corps, then another, attacked the Confederates and was checked. Then, in the afternoon, Burnside's corps crossed Antietam Creek, attacked Lee's right and was, like the others, driven back. Here the battle ended, in a draw.

Antietam was a slugging match, in which McClellan, once again, never pressed his advantage but attacked his enemy piecemeal and, when at last Lee retired, failed to chase him and destroy his army. Shaw wrote, "The result of the battle was that we remained in possession of the field, and the enemy drew off undisturbed. Whether that is all we wanted, I don't know; but I should think not." In fact, neither side was undisturbed. Each had lost about 11,500 men—in Lee's case, one quarter of his army. Lincoln openly expressed disgust at a general who would not pursue his enemy, calling McClellan's army, ". . . the general's bodyguard."

Shaw wrote that General Mansfield had been killed. "He had been with us only three days, but everyone liked him; he took more personal interest in the comfort and welfare of the men than any commander the corps has had." Almost as an afterthought, Shaw wrote, "I was struck once by a spent ball in the neck, which bruised, but didn't break the skin." He wrote about a friend of his, the brave and popular Lieutenant Colonel Wilder Dwight. "I suppose you know that poor Dwight is dead; he was very anxious to live until his Father and Mother could get here. He is a great loss to all of us, as well as to them; it will

be a terrible blow to his Mother, as he was her favorite son. . . . "
Chaplain Alonzo Quint, who wrote a history of the Second, was
with Dwight just after he was hit. Quint remembered how
Dwight took his fate. "'Mind, I don't flinch a hair,' said he, while
lying on a stretcher; sending the surgeon to relieve the
wounded, or telling his attendants to give water to the thirsty
men."

Shaw remembered, "At last night came on, and, with the
exception of an occasional shot from the outposts, all was quiet.
The crickets chirped, and the frogs croaked, just as if nothing
had happened all day long, and presently the stars came out
bright, and we lay down among the dead, and slept soundly
until daylight."

Lincoln, tired of waiting for a decisive Union victory, was
quick to seize on the outcome at Antietam to avert British
recognition of the Confederacy and to turn away increasing
criticism of his lukewarm attitude toward black enlistment in
the Union army. At noon, on September 22, he called his
cabinet to order. All were present. So as to relieve the tension,
he read aloud a story—*High-Handed Outrage at Utica*—by
humorist Artemis Ward, which he thought immensely funny.
Then he grew serious as he said, "When the rebel army was at
Frederick I determined as soon as it should be driven out of
Maryland to issue a proclamation of emancipation."

Lincoln had taken many months to consider and to write the
document that he was about to read. In 1861, as war began,
the pressures on the chief executive to free the slaves had been
many, various and powerful. Precedent weighed heavily on the
side of early action. European countries that had once engaged
in the sale of human flesh—notably England, Holland, France,
Spain and Portugal—had long since outlawed the slave trade.
Russia, whose serfs had been set free by Czar Alexander II in
1861, no longer tolerated slavery. In many states and several
territories in the United States slavery was illegal, as it was in
Canada, Mexico and in French and British colonies in the
Atlantic and Caribbean. In the Western Hemisphere, only in
Brazil and Cuba had slavery lasted past the middle of the
century. In tolerating and supporting slavery, the United
States had lagged behind.

As war began, religious activists, especially Quakers, who
had long worked to end slavery, petitioned Lincoln to abolish

it by decree. Lincoln's vice president and members of his cabinet had urged him to emancipate the slaves. Generals, senators and congressmen told Lincoln that without its slaves the Confederacy would soon collapse.

Charles Sumner, the senator from Massachusetts who had been cruelly beaten by Southern Congressman Preston Brooks, talked often to the president. In May 1861, he took an evening drive with Lincoln through the streets of Washington, during which he told the president that he understood his caution but implored him to strike swiftly when the time was right. After the first defeat at Bull Run, Sumner voiced his opinion that the time had come at last. Lincoln disagreed. He was convinced that he must have a military victory before issuing his edict.

Frederick Douglass, soon to play a key role in the recruiting of the Fifty Fourth, supported Lincoln but, like Sumner, urged immediate emancipation. In May 1861, Douglass said, "The Union cause will never prosper till the war assumes an Anti-Slavery attitude and the Negro is enlisted on the loyal side." Following John Brown's banner, Douglass saw a tidal wave of liberated slaves overwhelming slavery.

By the spring of 1862, Lincoln was determined soon to use every means at his command to forestall Britain's diplomatic recognition of the Confederacy and to neutralize the key role of slaves in supporting the Confederacy. In response to these imperatives, he started writing a proclamation of emancipation during the first week in June—three months before Antietam. He went almost every day to the telegraph office of the War Department to read dispatches on the progress of the fighting. It was there that he wrote the first draft of his edict.

Thomas Eckert, in charge of the office, let Lincoln use the desk. On the first day, Lincoln wrote very little. Later, he wrote more but still spent a lot of time reflecting. Eckert remembered that, for minutes at a time, Lincoln followed the activities of a family of large spiders that had been allowed to weave a web above the desk. Eckert kept the document in a locked drawer of the desk but never read it. Vice President Hannibal Hamlin was probably the first to read this early draft, of which no copy now exists. The men talked behind locked doors. Lincoln spoke first. "Mr. Hamlin, you have been repeatedly urging me to issue a proclamation of emancipation freeing the slaves. I have concluded to yield to your advice in the matter and that of other friends, at the same time, as I may say, following my own judgment. Now listen to me as I read this paper." When Hamlin liked what he heard, Lincoln urged, "At least you can make some suggestions." At last, Hamlin did suggest some minor changes but later said that, in essence, it was entirely Lincoln's work, ". . . and no one else can claim any credit whatsoever in connection with it."

On September 22, after he had read the preliminary Emancipation Proclamation to the members of his cabinet, Lincoln allowed further minor changes to be made, then released it to the press. In its first important paragraph, the edict stated, "That on the 1st day of January, A.D. 1863, all persons held as slaves within any State or designated part of a State the people whereof shall then be in rebellion against the United States shall be then, thenceforward, and forever free. . . . "

In composing this important document, Lincoln had compromised once again. He failed to include the border states and parts of states then occupied by Union forces. Many people in the North pointed out that in states and territories where it did apply it could not be enforced. Frederick Douglass, in no mood to quibble, said of the proclamation, after it was issued on January 1, 1863, "I hail it as the doom of Slavery in all the States. I hail it as the end of all that miserable statesmanship, which has for sixty years juggled and deceived the people, by professing to reconcile what is irreconcilable."

The issuance of the Emancipation Proclamation brought great joy to black Americans. In Washington, free black minister Henry Turner grabbed the last remaining tattered copy of *The Washington Evening Star,* which contained the final text. The minister, pursued by people who had been denied a copy, ran down Pennsylvania Avenue,

> . . . and when the people saw me coming with the paper in my hand they raised a shouting cheer that was almost deafening. As many as could get around me lifted me to a great platform, and I started to read the proclamation. I had run the best end of a mile, I was out of breath and could not read. Mr. Hinton, to whom I handed the paper, read it with great force and clearness. . . . Men squealed, women fainted, dogs barked, white and colored people shook hands, songs were sung, and by this time cannons began to fire at the navy-yard, and follow in the wake of

the roar that had for some time been going on behind the
White House. . . . Great processions of colored and white
men marched to and fro and congratulated President
Lincoln on his proclamation. . . . It was indeed a time of
times, and a half time, nothing like it will ever be seen
again in this life.

The immediate effect of Lincoln's proclamation was to en-
courage free black men and former slaves to join the fight to
save the Union and so to do away with slavery. "And I further
declare and make known that such persons of suitable condition will be received into the armed services of the United
States to garrison forts, positions, stations, and other places,
and to man vessels of all sorts in said service." This provision
of the edict was to lead directly to the organization of the Fifty
Fourth and to Shaw's appointment as its colonel.

5

NOW THE FLAG SHALL BE UNFURLED
1863

On February 3, 1863 Shaw was in winter quarters at Stafford Courthouse in Virginia. On that day, his father visited him. Following a long and tiring trip to Washington and a voyage down the cold Potomac, Francis Shaw walked three miles on a frozen, rutted road to his son's camp, which had become a sort of shantytown. The elder Shaw warmed his hands by a camp stove, then handed Shaw a letter from John Andrew, governor of Massachusetts, asking him to take command of what was to be the first black regiment recruited in the Northeast.

Commonwealth of Massachusetts
Executive Department, Boston
January 30, 1863

Captain Robert G. Shaw
2nd Reg. Mass. Vol. Inf.

Captain,

I am about to organize in Massachusetts a Colored Regiment as part of the volunteer quota of this State—the commissioned officers to be white men. I have today written your father expressing to him my sense of the importance of this undertaking, and requesting him to forward to you this letter, in which I offer to you the Commission of Colonel over it. The Lieutenant Colonelcy

I have offered to Captain Hallowell of the Twentieth Massachusetts Regiment. It is important to the organization of this regiment that I should receive a reply to this offer at the earliest day consistent with your ability to arrive at a deliberate conclusion on the subject.

> Respectfully and very truly yours,
> John A. Andrew
> *Governor of Massachusetts*

The importance of this letter that had prompted Francis Shaw to deliver it in person. The younger Shaw read the letter and expressed reluctance to take on so great a responsibility. His father, who had guessed that his son might hesitate, reasoned with him gently.

Francis Shaw slept on a cot in his son's cabin, while Shaw lay awake. Later, William James spoke about what may have been Shaw's thoughts that restless night. "In this new negro-soldier venture, loneliness was certain, ridicule inevitable, failure possible; and Shaw was only twenty-five; and although he had stood among the bullets at Cedar Mountain and Antietam, he had till then been walking socially on the sunny side of life."

More important to Shaw than his social status or the possibility of failure in this pioneering venture was his profound attachment to his regiment. He had shared with his fellow officers long months of inactivity, interspersed with short periods of danger. When soldiers, who have strengthened their friendships at leisure go together into battle—see each other tested, sometimes save each other's lives and watch their comrades fall in combat—these friendships often rise to devotion. It must have been hard for Shaw to think of breaking ties like this.

In any case, by morning, Shaw had decided to refuse Andrew's offer. His father telegraphed the news to his mother, "Rob declines. I think rightly."

Shaw's mother wrote to Andrew, "This decision has caused me the bitterest disappointment I have ever experienced. . . . " She went on to say that, if her son had accepted this great trust, "It would have been the proudest moment of my life and I could have died satisfied that I had not lived in vain. This being the truth, you will believe that I have shed bitter tears at his refusal." Then, she added, "I do not understand it unless from a habit inherited from his Father of self-distrust in his own capabilities."

As it happened, Francis Shaw left his son in Virginia in an agony of indecision. Like many heroes throughout history, Shaw embarked on his final course of action with misgivings. He was beset by doubts, not so much about loneliness or ridicule as about his capacity suddenly to become a colonel in command of *any* regiment, much less a pioneering one.

It is more difficult to judge factors that attracted him toward acceptance of this extraordinary trust. His mother's eagerness to see him take up a great cause, to see him risk his life for it, influenced him, and Copeland's views no doubt had their effect on him, but it would not be accurate to say that, at this stage, Shaw was propelled by a desire to fight and die for oppressed Americans.

This was, indeed, the decision of Shaw's life. The strongest factor weighing in the balance must have been what his mother called self-distrust, because, after he had talked to his commanding officer and resolved his doubts about his competence, he changed his mind. On February 6, he telegraphed his acceptance.

About his new assignment, Shaw wrote to Anna Kneeland Haggerty, a young woman living in New York, to whom he was by then engaged. "At any rate I shall not be frightened out of it by its unpopularity; and I hope you won't care if it is made fun of. . . . I feel convinced I shall never regret having taken this step . . . for while I was undecided I felt ashamed of myself, as if I were cowardly." He closed, "With great love, (more every day). . . . "

Alone, Shaw traveled north, stopping in New York for visits with Annie and his family. His fiancée—almost two years older than he—appeared to be a perfect partner for him. Like Shaw, she came from a privileged family. Her round face was youthful, her expression soft and kind, revealing what was probably a serene intelligence. In accordance with her wishes, Shaw destroyed her letters to him but we know that she was a loyal, loving person.

In Boston Shaw met John Andrew, a plump and energetic man with bright blue eyes and a head of curly hair, who had been inaugurated in 1861 and was to serve until 1865. Andrew

Shaw as colonel of the Fifty Fourth. This photograph was taken while the regiment was in training. (Massachusetts Historical Society)

had been among the first to send troops to the defense of Washington. Shaw wrote, "I took a long drive with the Governor and liked him very much. He is not only a liberal-minded philanthropist, but a man of practical good sense."

Andrew was a man who had campaigned energetically for permission to recruit the Fifty Fourth and, in the face of many obstacles, was to work persistently to maintain the highest standards for the regiment and to fight for equal rights and equal pay for its men.

Born in Windham, Maine, Andrew was something of a prodigy. When he was in his early teens, his mother died. The loss cut deep and revealed in the boy a great capacity for tenderness and sympathy, as expressed in his attention to the remaining members of his family—his father, younger brother and two sisters. He was a fun-loving boy and, though he admired the eloquence of the preachers in his neighborhood, he taught himself to mimic them, giving sermons for his friends.

In Andrew's case, the boy was indeed the father of the man. He was a spellbinding speaker and a winning storyteller. He became a skillful lawyer and impassioned politician. One of his law partners said that Andrew let his work pile up, then attacked it like a man possessed and dispatched it in no time. He was honest, forthright and beguiling. He soon became a fearless abolitionist and gave brilliant and effective speeches against the provisions of the Fugitive Slave Act of 1850 and the decision in the Dred Scott case—a decision of the U.S. Supreme Court in which one inflammatory and far-reaching element was Chief Justice Roger B. Taney's declaration that black people, whether slave or free, were not, and never could become, full citizens of the United States.

Although Andrew never quite approved of John Brown's methods, he gave money and encouragement to Brown. After Brown's raid on Harper's Ferry, Andrew did assert that Brown's course of action was indefensible—except on grounds of insanity—but celebrated Brown's extraordinary qualities and gave money to a fund for his defense. After further legal action on behalf of John Brown became impossible, Andrew helped to raise money for Brown's family. At a meeting for that purpose, he declared, "John Brown himself is right."

Andrew gave Shaw an office in the State House so that he could do the paperwork connected to the organizing of the regiment. Though Shaw was a conspicuous and unassailable representative of Andrew's policies, the governor soon saw that Shaw was not a public speaker and asked other people to do most of the recruiting. More officers than were needed had applied for positions in the Fifty Fourth and, while Andrew concentrated on recruitment of enlisted men, Shaw sifted through applications for commissions.

While Shaw worked at the State House, he lived with relatives at 44 Beacon Street and walked the several hundred yards between his office and the house. Shaw hated what he called his, ". . . furnace-heated work." He wrote his fiancée, in New York. "Do write often, Annie dear, for I need a word occasionally from those whom I love, to keep up my courage."

TO COLORED MEN.

54th REGIMENT!

MASSACHUSETTS VOLUNTEERS,

OF

AFRICAN DESCENT!

$100 BOUNTY!

At the expiration of the term of service.

PAY, $13 A MONTH!

AND

STATE AID TO FAMILIES.

RECRUITING OFFICE,

 Cor. Cambridge & North Russell Sts., Boston.

Lieut. J. W. M. APPLETON, Recruiting Officer.

J. E. FARWELL & Co., Steam Job Printers, No. 37 Congress Street, Boston.

This broadside was probably the first poster used in recruiting men for the Fifty Fourth, the first black regiment from the Northeast. Lieutenant J. W. M. Appleton, a native of Boston, Massachusetts, was the regiment's first recruiting officer. (From the collection of the author)

Before Shaw arrived in Boston, a commission had been given to Bostonian John W. M. Appleton, a hollow-cheeked, full-bearded man, who began recruiting in a small black community on the north slope of Beacon Hill, where he enlisted one scant company. James W. Grace, commissioned February 10, recruited in New Bedford, where large numbers of free black Americans, some of whom had come to America from the Azores, lived. Grace—handsome, youthful, a native of New Bedford—paid a price for his success. People shouted at him in the street and his young son was teased unmercifully in school because his father was recruiting black men to fight against white men.

Despite the problems they encountered, these young officers held their ground. One of them voiced an interesting view of his decision to serve under Shaw. Lieutenant William H. Simkins wrote,

> This is no hasty conclusion, no blind leap of an enthusiast, but the result of much hard thinking. It will not be at first, and probably not for a long time, an agreeable position, for many reasons too evident to state. . . . Then this is nothing but an experiment after all; but an experiment that I think it high time we should try, an experiment which, the sooner we prove fortunate the sooner we can count upon an immense number of hardy troops . . . , an experiment which the sooner we prove unsuccessful, the sooner we shall establish an important truth and rid ourselves of a false hope.

As it turned out, there were not enough able-bodied volunteers in all of Massachusetts to fill the ranks and, in fact, there were difficulties in the Northeast as a whole. A booming war economy had brought good jobs and a measure of prosperity to Northern black Americans. Some asked, "Why trade a good job for what at best would be an uncertain future?" After all, captured black fighting men might be shot or sold into slavery and it was decreed that, at first, they could not serve as officers, a restriction many found insulting. However, in response to the charge that black men would cut and run at the first sound of cannon fire, many saw an opportunity to demonstrate that they would fight, and die if necessary, for a government that had promised to proclaim their brothers ". . . thenceforth and forever free."

*Frederick Douglass in his forties—as he looked at the time of recruit-
ment of the Fifty Fourth. Douglass himself applied for a commission in
the Union army but was unable to obtain one. He was active in recruiting free black men for the Fifty Fourth. His first recruit was his son,
Lewis Douglass, who became the regiment's sergeant major. Lewis's
younger brother Charles joined later. Both saw action at Fort Wagner.
Both survived.* (From the collection of the author)

In order to accelerate recruiting efforts, Andrew appointed George Luther Stearns to head what became the Black Committee, people who would carry their recruiting efforts far and wide. Stearns—a wealthy Massachusetts manufacturer—was a lean dynamic man of 54, who had been a close associate and promoter of the fortunes of Charles Sumner, John Andrew and John Brown and had provided funds for Brown's raid on Harper's Ferry. As he formed the Black Committee, Stearns had the help of John Murray Forbes, whose son had talked so long to Shaw on the eve of the battle of Antietam. Forbes—a brilliant and forceful man—had made a large fortune through investment in the China trade and railroading in the West. He too had supported John Brown's activities and had consistently promoted the recruitment of black regiments. These two were joined by other men of similar persuasion, among them Shaw's father, who was soon to be active in recruiting in New York.

Stearns was quick to enlist the help of black leaders in his native state and New York and Pennsylvania. First among them was Frederick Douglass, then a resident of Rochester, New York, and publisher of a monthly abolitionist newspaper. Douglass, who was in his mid-forties, was vigorous and youthful. Born a slave in Maryland, on the eastern shore of Chesapeake Bay, he was at first a privileged servant, given opportunities that few slaves were ever given, but soon he became rebellious and was sold to Hugh Auld, who lived in a modest house in the Fells Point section of Baltimore, a shipbuilding neighborhood. Broad-shouldered Master Hugh, a ship's carpenter, was as mean and unapproachable as his wife was sympathetic and encouraging. Douglass long remembered an occasion when his mistress told him gently, "Look up child. Don't be afraid."

In Fells Point, Douglass saw half-starved slaves driven through the narrow streets in chains. Touched deeply by their silent suffering, he resolved to escape and fight against the degradation suffered by his brothers. As he grew to manhood, his intelligence and force of character frightened Master Hugh who hired him out to Edward Covey, a professional slave-breaker. Under Covey, Douglass suffered great cruelty. Later, he remembered that one day, despite great weakness brought on by a lack of food and by hard labor, he stood up to Covey. "This battle with Mr. Covey was the turning point in my career. I was a changed man after that fight. I was nothing before, I was a man now . . . with renewed determination to be a free man. . . . The gratification afforded by this triumph was a full compensation for whatever else might follow, even death itself. . . . "

In response to Douglass's rebellion, Auld decided to sell him to a plantation owner in a Southern state but instead, probably at the urging of his wife, hired him out once again, this time to the owner of a shipyard, where Douglass found himself in competition with white laborers, many of whom hated blacks. At last, in 1838, he escaped to New York, followed soon by Anna Murray, a free black woman who loved him and would soon become his wife. The couple married in New York and continued north, to New England, where Douglass kept his promise to himself and began his long career as an abolitionist, a career that made him the most influential black American of his time, a great black spokesman widely known in his own country and in foreign lands as well.

In his effort to recruit men for the Fifty Fourth, Douglass spoke with the passion of a man who had felt the sting of slavery. In Rochester, on March 2, he appealed to an audience of young black men.

> When the first Rebel cannon shattered the walls of Sumter, and drove away its starving garrison, I predicted that the war then and there inaugurated would not be fought out entirely by white men. Every month's experience during these two dreary years has confirmed that opinion. A war undertaken and brazenly carried on for the perpetual enslavement of colored men, calls logically and loudly upon colored men to help suppress it.

In his compelling voice, he urged, "I have implored the imperilled nation to unchain against her foes her powerful black hand." In persuading his black brothers to enlist, he said, "The tide is at flood that leads on to fortune. From east to west, from north to south the sky is written all over with 'now or never.' Liberty won by white men would lack half its lustre. Who would be free themselves must strike the blow." He declared,

> I will not argue. To do so implies hesitation and doubt, and you do not hesitate. You do not doubt. The day dawns—the

morning star is bright upon the horizon! The iron gate of
our prison stands half open. One gallant rush from the
North will fling it wide open, while four millions of our
brothers and sisters shall march out into Liberty!

Although Douglass never wore a uniform, his son Lewis was
his first recruit. Lewis became sergeant major of the regiment
and was soon joined by his brother Charles.

In Philadelphia, which had a larger black population than
any other city in the North, Morris Hallowell and his son
Edward rounded up a company of healthy men and, in order to
avoid harassment, sent them north in small groups, in the dead
of night. Andrew encouraged Stearns to recruit in all the
Northern states and Canada, and Stearns, responding, was
incredibly successful. A New York conservative wrote scorn-
fully of Andrew's efforts. "His crimping sergeants will shortly
turn up in Egypt, competing with Napoleon for the next cargo
of Nubians."

Andrew ignored such comments and, as it went off to war,
the Fifty Fourth was to have in its ranks men from all six New
England states, 10 other states and Canada. So successful were
recruiting efforts that Shaw's second in command, Norwood P.
Hallowell, was soon to take command of a following black
regiment—the Massachusetts Fifty Fifth—and was to be replaced by his brother Edward N. Hallowell.

In early March, Shaw left Boston and took personal command in the training of his regiment at Camp Meigs, at
Readville, a place of open fields and lightly wooded hills—on
the Boston and Providence railroad line—in what is now sub-
urban Boston.

Massachusetts Surgeon General Dale had set high standards
for acceptance of men for the regiment and, as a consequence,
Shaw's work was rewarding. Shaw wrote his father, "If the
success of the Fifty Fourth gives you so much pleasure, I shall
have no difficulty giving you good words of it. . . . " He praised
the recruits, noted their adaptability to soldiering. "There is
not the least doubt that we shall leave the State with as good
a regiment as any that has marched."

Others noted the exceptional *esprit de corps* of the men of the
regiment and, in one of his reports, Dale wrote, "The barracks,
cookhouses, and kitchens far surpassed in cleanliness any I

have ever witnessed, and were models of neatness and good order. On parade, their appearance was marked with great neatness of personal appearance as concerned dress and the good condition in which their arms and accoutrements were kept."

At first Shaw was shy and aloof. Like many Northerners, he had had little contact with black people, but he was quick to learn and quick to change. At first, in describing his enlisted men to friends of his, he blandly referred to them as *darkies, nigs* or *niggers*—terms that may have had a slightly different flavor then than they do now but were, nevertheless, condescending and insulting. His condescension took a familiar form as he declared himself, ". . . perfectly astonished at the general intelligence these darkies display."

Later, as he started to relate to his men as individuals, he came to regard them with respect, then affection, and, from that time on, his letters to his friends contained no offensive references.

Shaw's men were beautifully equipped, and he provided them with comforts not available to men in white regiments. There was talk, at first and later, of equipping them with pikes—pointed shafts resembling spears—instead of rifles, but Shaw scoffed at such suggestions and, before they went to war, the men were issued Enfield rifles.

While serving in Virginia, Shaw had written, "There are cowards everywhere & there is probably very little difference between regiments in this respect. Their behavior depends almost entirely on the discipline." As he trained the Fifty Fourth he enforced standard military discipline. Up before dawn, his enlisted men retired soon after dark, having cleaned their barracks, drilled, made forced marches with full packs and engaged in bayonet practice. As the clear and mournful notes of taps sounded in the winter air and died away, they were expected to lie still and go to sleep.

Most reporters praised Shaw, but hostile journalists reported that both officers and men were subjected to harsh punishments. One said that offenders were too often locked up in the guardhouse—the regimental jail. Another witness argued, "The guard house is seldom occupied." A scholar recently reported that, ". . . the records are incomplete as to exactly the punishments inflicted."

Shaw wrote to his mother about negative reports. "One trouble that I have anticipated has begun: namely, complaints from outsiders, of undue severity; but I shall continue to do what is right in that particular, and you may be perfectly certain that any reports of cruelty are entirely untrue." Referring to his men, he said, "I have treated them much more mildly than we did the men of the Second."

In fact, Shaw was proud of his growing regiment and became its protector. When it was still only at half strength, Stanton, Lincoln's secretary of war, asked that the men already trained be sent south, to join regiments made up of contrabands—escaped or abandoned slaves. Shaw didn't want to mix his hand-picked, disciplined and dedicated soldiers with the men of what he thought were raggle-taggle aggregations. He protested, saying that his regiment must reach full strength, go to war as a unit, rise or fall on its merits. Andrew, who agreed, saw that Shaw had his way.

Lieutenant Colonel Hallowell, Shaw's second-in-command, was a son of a prominent Philadelphia family. He was described by Massachusetts wartime governor John A. Andrew as, ". . . true as steel to the cause of humanity, as well as the flag of the Country." After Shaw's death and after Hallowell recovered from a wound sustained in the July 18 attack on Fort Wagner, he became commander of the Fifty Fourth. (Massachusetts Historical Society)

Some of Shaw's men were homesick. Others had family problems. Some went absent without leave, an offense that, in some cases, might have justified execution. Deserters were returned to camp and were punished, but no man was treated brutally and none was shot.

At first, Readville was cold and damp. When icy winds raised snowdrifts on the parade ground, the men drilled in empty barracks and warmed themselves by wood stoves. There was little opportunity for recreation, but the men were young and spirited. They sang and danced in the barracks and, as the weather moderated, went outside and played baseball.

As spring approached, Shaw wanted desperately to marry Annie Haggerty. He carried on a war of words with his mother, who pressured him to postpone the ceremony. Shaw held firm. "For the sake of Annie's and my own peace of mind, I want it."

Annie came to Readville and stayed in a boardinghouse, close to camp. There Shaw spend long hours with her in the parlor. Charles Russell Lowell and Shaw's sister Josephine—also engaged to one another—had rooms at the same boardinghouse and the four spent some pleasant evenings with each other. Shaw wrote, "I see Annie every evening, almost, and feel more and more satisfied every day, as I learn to know her better."

On May 2, the couple married in the Church of the Ascension, on Fifth Avenue at Tenth Street, in New York City. They spent a brief honeymoon in Lenox, Massachusetts, where Shaw wrote a short letter to his parents. "The country is looking beautifully here; the trees are beginning to bud, and the grass to grow green." He wrote to his sister Josephine, "I have been in quite an angelic mood ever since we got here. . . . "

On May 7, as he and his wife prepared to go back to Readville, Shaw became depressed but, back in camp, he was greeted warmly and found his soldiers in high spirits as they drilled in preparation for the ceremony that would mark the end of training.

May 18 dawned bright and clear. At 11:00, Shaw's voice rang out, bringing officers and men to attention. All were resplendent in clean uniforms adorned with polished brass and gleaming leather. Gathered on the parade ground were large numbers of both black and white Bostonians and promoters of the regiment—Garrison, Douglass, Phillips, Stearns, Forbes, and an array of distinguished military figures. Shaw's father and young bride were present, but Shaw's mother hadn't felt that she was strong enough to make the journey.

Governor Andrew shared the reviewing stand with Shaw and his senior officers. He gave a long speech during which he turned to Shaw and said, "I know not, Mr. Commander, when, in all human history, to any given thousand men in arms there has been committed a work at once so proud, so precious. . . . " As he handed Shaw the stars and stripes, he proclaimed, "Wherever its folds shall be unfurled, it will mark the path of glory."

6

PATH OF GLORY
1863

At dawn on May 28, Shaw and his regiment left Readville, went by train to Boston and paraded through the streets. The sky above the brick and gray stone houses was bright blue. The leaves of the trees on Boston Common and in the Public Garden stirred restlessly in a warm breeze. Patrick Gilmore's marching band heralded the arrival of the Fifty Fourth. Following a trail of sprightly music, Shaw—on his best mount, his back straight, his unsheathed sword held at his side—led his regiment across the paving stones.

As Shaw swept around a corner, he saw a close friend and ally of his parents. Later, in his diary, the man wrote about his fleeting glimpse of Shaw. "I got from him that lovely, almost heavenly smile. . . . "

Several companies of police were in reserve, to put down expected rioting, but they were never needed. Captain Luis Emilio, who survived to write a history of the Fifty Fourth, noted that, ". . . not an insulting word was heard, or an unkind remark made."

It must be said that, while the regiment was applauded all along the route of march, there were those who frowned on it. The same people who for years had laughed at and reviled the abolitionists turned their backs or pulled down their windowshades.

Most of Boston's Irish citizens were outraged—as were the Irish in New York—by the prospect of a rise in social status for a people with whom they were constantly in competition for employment. An editorial in the *Boston Pilot* remarked that "there is not an American living that should not blush at the plan of making such a race the defenders of the national fame and power."

Former slave Harriet Jacobs—who had suffered greatly in the South—watched as the regiment passed by. She wrote later, "How my heart swelled with the thought that my poor oppressed race were to strike a blow for Freedom!"

William Lloyd Garrison, who watched the passage of the regiment at Wendell Phillips's house on Essex Street, was so affected that his cheeks were streaked with tears. As rank after rank of soldiers moved uphill toward the State House, accompanied by Gilmore's Marching Band, the crowd stirred. Applause broke out. As Shaw and his smartly uniformed men appeared, the people lining the sidewalks began to cheer. The cheers became tumultuous, reminding Shaw of his long march down Broadway, in New York, two years before.

At the steps of the State House, Shaw was greeted by the governor and his staff, who joined the soldiers in their march down Beacon Street. Shaw's father waited on the Common with fellow members of the Black Committee while the other members of Shaw's family sat on a shallow balcony at 44 Beacon Street. As Shaw drew abreast of the elegant brick house, he glanced up at their faces. His sister Ellen, who watched with the others, wrote later, "I was not quite eighteen when the regiment sailed. My mother, Rob's wife, my sisters and I were on the balcony to see the regiment go by, and when Rob, riding at its head, looked up and kissed his sword, his face was as the face of an angel and I felt perfectly sure he would never come back."

The regiment moved down the hill, entering Boston Common by the Charles Street gate. On the Common, there were further ceremonies. Every member of the Black Committee was on hand. Pacifist and poet John Greenleaf Whittier stood in the crowd. Whittier's heartbeat quickened as the band struck up again and the regiment marched toward the West Street gate, but he wrote no verse about the regiment or its commander, ". . . lest I should indirectly give a new impulse to war." When peace came at last, he did write to Lydia Maria Child, "The only regiment I ever looked upon during the war was the 54th Massachusetts on its departure for the South. I can never forget the scene as Colonel Shaw rode at the head of his men. The very flower of grace and chivalry, he seemed to me beau-

The Saint-Gaudens memorial to Shaw and the men who fought and died with him. Saint-Gaudens worked on the monument for 14 years. His major works and many of his studies still exist. The Shaw memorial stands on Boston Common, opposite the Massachusetts State House. It was unveiled on May 31, 1897. (The Houghton Library, Harvard University)

tiful and awful, as an angel of God come down to lead the host of freedom to victory."

At Battery Wharf, the regiment filed aboard the new and comfortable military transport *De Molay*. The families of many soldiers lived so far from Boston that they couldn't be on hand that day, but Frederick Douglass, who had come from Rochester, made the most of the occasion, staying aboard the *De Molay* as it sailed across the harbor. He returned to Boston on a tug and, in view of the awful carnage of the first two years of war, must have watched with mixed emotions as he saw his two sons go off to war, as the ship grew ever smaller and, at last, disappeared.

The Fifty Fourth was under orders to report to General David Hunter, whose headquarters were on Hilton Head, one of a chain of islands on the low sandy coast of South Carolina, separated from the mainland and each other by the lazy rivers, sounds and estuaries of the region. The Fifty Fourth would soon go into camp on St. Helena, just across Port Royal Sound from Hilton Head, but first the regiment would make an unwelcome detour.

The voyage south was marked by little danger but, even though the food was good, the motion of the ship made some men sick. Hallowell's mare died at sea and was lowered overboard, while Shaw's three horses only lost a little weight. On June 3 the *De Molay* passed Fort Sumter and proceeded south toward Hilton Head.

Six months or so after the beginning of hostilities, Lincoln had approved a plan to invade the Sea Islands of South Carolina. Foresight might have enabled some of the aristocratic Southerners who owned plantations on the islands to carry off most of their harvest and their treasure, but they hadn't quite believed that anyone would interfere with their harvest. One South Carolinian had asked, "Would any sane nation make war on cotton?" When the invaders did arrive, on November 7, 1861, Charlestonian James L. Petigrew, who loved both his native state and the Union, said, "On the islands a discovery is made which the inhabitants were slow in coming to, that in a war with an enemy that is master of the sea they are masters of nothing."

On June 3, the *De Molay* crossed the bar and made for Hilton Head. Port Royal Sound, used as an anchorage for the blockading fleet, must have been a breathtaking sight that day. Emilio reported, "The steamer crossed the grand harbor with some seventy sail moored upon its waters, including the frig-ates *Wabash* and *Vermont,* a monitor, several gunboats, and a French steamer. . . . " The *De Molay* docked at the end of a long pier, where Union engineers had built a shipyard and sheds and warehouses that held coal, lumber, food and armament for the Department of the South.

Shaw disembarked, walked the length of the pier and re-ported to the plantation house where General Hunter lived and worked. Hunter was a strange mix. He was an abolitionist who knew and had worked with Lincoln. Arrogant and independent, he had issued his own version of an emancipation proclamation, on May 9, 1862, which in part had said, "The persons in these three states—Georgia, Florida, and South Carolina—heretofore held as slaves are . . . declared forever free." Lincoln had dis-avowed this proclamation on the grounds that Hunter had ex-ceeded his authority. Worse than Hunter's issuance of unauthorized decrees was his handling of the contrabands—es-caped or abandoned slaves. Hunter had caused some of these to be seized in the fields, giving them no chance to refuse to serve in what were supposed to be volunteer regiments, and no time to let their families know where they were going. Shaw wrote that "there is some talk of his being removed."

When the *De Molay* had been refueled and Hunter had re-viewed Shaw's troops, the steamer took the regiment to Port Royal Island. The Fifty Fourth spent four days encamped near Beaufort, the only town of any size in the region. Shaw lent Hallowell a horse and the two rode into town. A curving street, sheltered by great spreading oaks and Spanish moss, embraced the waterfront. Long dominated by Robert Barnwell Rhett, whose heirs were described by a neighbor as unscrupulous and malignant, Beaufort had been a hotbed of secessionist activity. The houses on the waterway—tall and fronted by impressive porches—were then occupied by contrabands and Union soldiers.

In Beaufort, Shaw and Hallowell met Thomas Wentworth Higginson, long an abolitionist, then colonel of the First South Carolina Infantry, a regiment of contrabands. Higginson, a tall slightly awkward man of 39, looked more like a schoolmaster than someone who had tried to batter down a courthouse door to free a slave. The three men talked about the problems that confronted the commanders of black regiments. Afterward, Shaw wrote of Higginson, "I never saw one who put his whole heart into his work as he does; I was very much impressed with his open-heartedness and purity of character." Later, Higginson said of Shaw, "I should have known Shaw anywhere by his resemblance to his kindred, nor did it take long to perceive that he shared their habitual truthfulness and courage." He observed that Shaw was a man possessed of quiet power.

Two days later Shaw met Colonel James Montgomery, a thin, bearded man in his late forties. Montgomery had met John Brown in 1858. At first, the two liked each other and agreed to cooperate in preventing the spread of slavery into Kansas Territory but, when Brown saw that Montgomery had what he called, ". . . ideas of his own," he began to dislike him. Despite this falling out, Montgomery supported Brown, giving fiery speeches and using threats of violence to intimidate proslavery settlers.

When Shaw met him, Montgomery was commander of the Second South Carolina Infantry, which, like the First, was made up of contrabands. Shaw wrote, "The bushwhacker Montgomery is a strange compound; he allows no swearing or drinking in his regiment, and is *anti-tobacco;* but he burns and destroys wherever he goes with great gusto, and looks as if he would have quite a taste for hanging people, whenever a suitable subject should offer." Shaw noted that Montgomery never raised his voice but that his face was frightening. He had a ". . . queer roll or glare in his eye."

Montgomery had just returned from what was thought to be a successful foray up the Combahee, a raid in which he had seized several hundred contrabands and destroyed some private property. In spite of Shaw's misgivings, he asked the Kansan if he could go with him on his next expedition to the mainland.

On the morning of June 9, the *De Molay* anchored in a quiet cove off St. Simons Island—on the Georgia coast, 30 miles or so by sea from Port Royal. In mounting heat, the Fifty Fourth was transferred in shifts to barges and taken upstream where it set up camp at Pike's Bluff, above Montgomery's camp.

Shaw knew something of the history of St. Simons. English cleric John Wesley, who had come to Georgia in 1735, had preached in a chapel there. On the island, in 1742, the British had defeated a small Spanish army in the Bloody Swamp. Shaw may or may not have known that the invading Spanish force had contained one regiment of blacks and another of mulattoes.

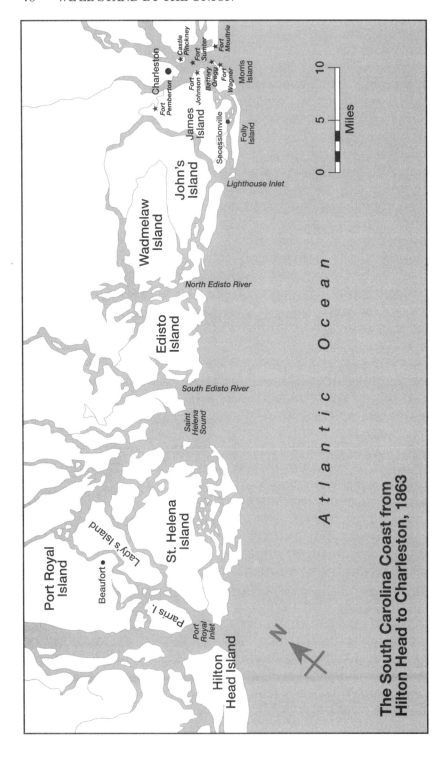

The South Carolina Coast from
Hilton Head to Charleston, 1863

On June 10, just after noon, a small shallow-draft transport brought Montgomery to Pike's Bluff. Standing on the deck of the steamer, he asked Shaw, "How soon can you be ready to start on an expedition?"

Shaw called back, "In half an hour."

Leaving a camp guard behind, Shaw and eight of his companies sailed downstream. The next day found the Fifty Fourth and five companies of the First Carolina Regiment in Doboy Sound, where they were joined by the gunboats *Harriet A. Weed* and *Paul Jones*.

Montgomery made it known that his objective was the town of Darien, on the Altamaha River and, moving up the Altamaha, his gunboats led the way firing on private houses. This irresponsible destruction worried Shaw who had seen as much of war as Montgomery but, in spite of having been fired on by townspeople in Winchester, was determined to spare non-combatants—old people, women, children.

The transports took the soldiers up the Atamaha to Darien, a town settled in the 18th century by immigrants from Inverness, Scotland. The main street was lined with graceful brick and wood-frame houses, mulberry and oak trees, three churches and a variety of public buildings. All was quiet. The mayor and most of the inhabitants had retreated to a ridge, a few miles west. Two white women and some slaves had stayed behind but were not armed and offered no resistance. Montgomery ordered that Shaw's men gather things that would be useful back in camp—livestock, resin, lumber, tools and lamps. A junior officer remembered later, "The plundering thus legitimized began." The men took the treasure of the town to the boats. They carted off paintings, mirrors, sofas, chairs, carpets, bedsteads, books and clothing. "A private would come along with a slate, a yard-stick, and a brace of chickens in one hand, and in the other hand a rope with a cow attached."

Shaw and Montgomery sat astride their horses, looking on. As their soldiers finished looting, Montgomery turned to Shaw and said softly, "I shall burn this town." When Shaw protested, Montgomery said that the Rebels must be ". . . swept away by the hand of God like the Jews of old."

Shaw, who was willing to be court martialed if necessary, continued to object, but Montgomery only smiled. At last, Shaw refused point-blank to have his men engage in the destruction of the town, but Montgomery quietly and firmly ordered some of Shaw's men to assist.

Knowing that their commander was opposed to the action, Shaw's soldiers went about the work half-heartedly, but Montgomery's men, all of whom had been slaves, took pleasure in their task and soon the whole town was on fire. Next, Montgomery ordered that the waterfront be set ablaze. In so doing, he risked the safety of the transports but somehow the ships were spared and, once loaded, left the docks and sailed back down the Altamaha, leaving Darien in ruins.

The Fifty Fourth returned to camp on St. Simons, where Shaw talked to Hallowell about the implications of the sacking of the town and wrote letters of protest—one to Governor Andrew and the other to Lieutenant Colonel Halpine, who was on Hunter's staff. Shaw wrote his wife that the action was ". . . as abominable a job as I ever had a share in." News of the raid was met with shock and dismay in the North and, when Lincoln heard about it, he was angry and dismissed his friend General Hunter.

Shaw took note of the features of St. Simons—the shell roads, the brilliant flowers and exotic birds. He met and talked to people who had been Pierce Butler's slaves, some of whom remembered Butler's wife, Fanny Kemble. In 1834, when she was only 25, Kemble had married Butler not knowing he owned slaves and, in 1838, had gone to Georgia with him. There, she kept a journal, where she recorded her impressions of the plight of the slaves. This journal—first published in 1863—helped expose the true nature of the institution Shaw was fighting to eradicate.

In long poetic passages, she described the beauties of her husband's islands, contrasting these delights with the practices of white people who were kinder to their animals than they were to their slaves. When she asked a woman who was turning soil with a spade and a hoe why plows weren't used, she was told that it was, "'cause horses more costly to keep than colored folks." Kemble talked to her husband about the flogging of a field hand named Theresa. "These discussions are terrible: they throw me into a perfect agony of distress for the slaves, whose position is utterly hopeless. . . . "

Another woman, having been flogged several times, described the process to her mistress, told how she had been fastened by the wrists to a branch or a beam, so that her toes just touched the ground, shift turned up and tied above her head and her back scored with leather thongs.

When she visited a sick woman, Kemble was outraged by conditions in the plantation infirmary. Its earthen floor was damp and ". . . was strewn with wretched women, who, but for their moans of pain, and uneasy restless motions, might very well have been taken for a mere heap of filthy rags. . . . " Moving from a room filled with smoke because the flue was clogged, she went to another room where there was no heat at all. She wrote, "The shutters being closed, the place was so dark that, on first entering it, I was afraid to stir lest I should fall over some of the deplorable creatures extended upon the floor. As soon as they perceived me, one cry of 'Oh Missis!' rang through the darkness. . . . The poor dingy supplicating sleepers upraised themselves as I cautiously advanced among them. . . . " One woman, so exhausted that she could barely speak, told her mistress that she was the mother of nine children. "There she lay, a mass of filthy tatters, without so much as a blanket under her or over her, on the bare earth in this chilly darkness. I promised them help and comfort, beds and blankets, and light and fire. . . . I wandered home, stumbling with crying as I went, and feeling so utterly miserable that I hardly knew were I was going. . . . "

Shaw never read Kemble's letters, but was touched by his encounters with some of the people who had known her. He wrote from St. Simons, "A deserted homestead is always a sad sight, but . . . we see that every such overgrown plantation, and empty house, is a harbinger of freedom for the slaves. . . . "

Hunter was replaced by Quincy Adams Gillmore, who decided to suspend what amounted to guerrilla action and give his attention to attacking Charleston, starting with outlying defenses—the forts and batteries on the south side of the harbor. First, he had to gain control of James Island, which adjoined Morris Island.

The Fifty Fourth was to become part of a large force that was gathering on St. Helena, which was encircled by green marshlands and protected from the sea by countless smaller islands. Soon after Shaw's arrival, there was trouble over pay. He wrote his father, "You may have heard, perhaps, that the coloured troops are to receive $10 instead of $13 per month; it is not yet decided that this regiment comes under the order; if it does, I shall refuse to allow them to be paid until I hear from Governor

Andrew." The Fifty Fourth was indeed included in the order—a clear violation of a promise made by Andrew at Readville that the men of the regiment would, in all particulars, be on the same footing as white soldiers. With the full support of his men, Shaw did refuse to have them paid but, as we will see, the fight over pay went on until the war was in its final stages.

When the landlords of the vast plantations on St. Helena had fled to the mainland, most of their slaves had stayed behind. Even many of the so-called Swonga People—house servants who composed a black aristocracy—had remained, willing to take a chance on the goodwill of the invaders.

Shortly after the Sea Islands had been occupied by Union troops, St. Helena had been chosen as the headquarters of what came to be called the Port Royal Experiment—an attempt by teachers from the North, most of them from Massachusetts and New York, to educate a people who had willfully been kept in ignorance and, for the most part, spoke a soft and musical dialect of their own—called Gullah—which was similar to a language spoken by tribes in West Africa.

In the fall of 1862, Charlotte Forten, standing on the deck of the steamship *United States,* had crossed the deep and placid waters of Port Royal Sound and had gone to live with seven other teachers in a plantation house on St. Helena. Forten was the only teacher who was black. Laura Towne, who supervised the crusading women and looked after their well-being, wrote that at first the Swonga People, some of whom kept house for the teachers, didn't know what to think of this educated woman, who in every way but one was like the others: "Aunt Becky required some coaxing to wait on her and do her room."

Soon, however, both house servants and field hands changed their minds. Higginson noted that the contrabands were impressed with Forten's manners and her skills; "When they heard her *play on the piano,* it quite put them down and all grew fond of her."

Shaw met Forten on the evening of July 2, when he went to the plantation house. He wrote, "She is quite pretty, remarkably well-educated, and a very interesting woman. She is decidedly the 'belle' here, and the officers, both of the army and navy, seem to think her society far preferable to that of the other ladies." In her diary, Forten wrote of Shaw, "To me, he seems a thoroughly lovable person."

Shaw had tea with the teachers, then went with them to a praise meeting. Shaw wrote, "The praying was done by an old, blind fellow who . . . seemed to throw his whole soul into it." After the praise meeting, Shaw and Forten went to what the island people called a shout—a dance that, like the Gullah language, had its roots in Africa. The performance troubled Forten, who thought it was barbaric, but Shaw found it interesting. He wrote, "They all walk and shuffle round in a ring, singing and chanting, while three or four stand in a corner and clap their hands to mark the time. At certain parts of the chorus, they all give a duck, the effect of which is very peculiar. . . . They sometimes keep it up all night. . . . "

On July 4, Shaw and Forten were together on what might have been her first truly happy Independence Day. Six years before, at 19, she had written, "The celebration of this day! What a mockery it is! My soul sickens of it." Shaw and the others stood on the grounds of a small Baptist church and listened to a sermon by a black preacher. Shaw wrote, "The gay dresses and turbans of the women made the sight very brilliant." He saw what was happening to the people of the island as proof of the justice of the Union cause.

> Can you imagine anything more wonderful than a colored abolitionist meeting on a South Carolina plantation? There were collected all the free slaves on this island . . . while two years ago their masters were still here, the lords of the soil and of them. Now they all own something themselves, go to school, to church, and work for wages!

A small boy read the Declaration of Independence, then the voices of the members of the congregation rose in celebration of the day of freedom. Shaw wrote his mother, "Miss Forten promised to write out the words of some of the hymns they sang, which I will send you." Later, Forten wrote of Shaw, "We all looked upon him with the deepest interest. There was something in his face finer, more exquisite than one often sees in a man's face, yet it was full of courage and decision. . . . How full of life and hope and lofty ambitions he was that night!"

Shaw saw her once again on the evening of July 6, when he and another officer entertained her and two of her colleagues at their camp. Some of Shaw's men sang songs for their guests, then Shaw and Forten talked at length. That night, before she went to bed, she lit her lamp and wrote in her diary, "Tonight, he helped me on my horse, and after carefully arranging the folds of my riding skirt, said, so kindly, 'Goodbye, if I don't see you again down here, I hope to see you at our house.'"

Shaw had met General Strong a week before and had liked him very much. He knew Strong was bound for Charleston and decided he would like to serve with him. He reported to his parents, "I wrote to General Strong this afternoon, and expressed my wish to be in his Brigade. . . . I want to get my men along side of white troops, and into a good fight, if there is to be one." He added that General Strong had sent him word that, ". . . he was very much disappointed at being ordered to leave us; so I thought it well to put into his head to try to get us back."

Shaw's letter was effective. Strong asked for the Fifty Fourth. Shaw wrote a short note to his sister Josephine. "We are ordered to Folly Island at an hour's notice, and if there is to be an attack on Charleston, shall have our share in it. We go in such a hurry, that we must leave everything behind but India-rubber blankets, and two days' rations."

The steamer *Chasseur,* with the Fifty Fourth aboard, ploughed north some 40 miles in stormy seas and arrived in Stono Inlet at 1:00 A.M., on July 9. Many men had been sick; all were tired.

The regiment was part of an army of 11,000 men under Gillmore who had planned a *coup de main*—an attack in force—against Morris Island and Fort Wagner. Having boarded the *Chasseur* in a rainstorm, the men slept in damp uniforms. That afternoon, the transport steamed up the Stono River with a monitor, two gunboats and a mortar schooner in attendance.

At dawn on July 10, still aboard the transport, Shaw heard the boom of cannon coming from Morris Island and, that day, news came that all of Morris Island south of Wagner was in Union hands. The mail brought the news of distant victories, at Vicksburg and Gettysburg. These good tidings raised Shaw's spirits and increased his eagerness to join the main force, under Strong.

At noon on July 11, Shaw took his regiment ashore on James Island, which was covered with underbrush. Shaw couldn't see his enemy so he sent out four companies to join a front line—then called a picket line. This detachment was commanded by blunt-featured, solid Captain Simkins, whose decision to serve in the Fifty Fourth had been the result of ". . . much hard thinking."

For several days, the men of the regiment lay in wait, guessing that their enemy was expecting reinforcements. During this inactive period, the Tenth Connecticut took up a hazardous position on the left, with its back to a swamp.

Before dark, one of Simkins's officers climbed to the roof of a small house and came back with the news that the Confederates were preparing to attack. At dawn, on July 16, enemy artillery hit one of the supporting gunboats, killing several sailors.

Shaw, in command of his main force, cantered along the line, telling his men to prepare for an attack. The pickets of the Fifty Fourth took the brunt of the assault. As luck had it, leading elements of the Confederate force charged the line where Simkins waited with his men. There was an awful moment when the young officer thought his men—under fire for the first time—might falter, but they knew that the soldiers of the Tenth Connecticut would be trapped and slaughtered if they didn't hold the line so they stood fast. What began as an exchange of rifle fire became hand-to-hand combat. Sergeant Peter Vogelsang was waiting for the enemy when it seemed that, all at once, ". . . one hundred Rebels were swarming about me." Vogelsang not only stood fast but advanced, taking with him his whole company.

Tall, strong Sergeant James Wilson had vowed never to retreat. As he shouted to his men to stand fast, five Confederates turned on him. He disabled three attackers and the others passed him by. He was charged by several mounted men and fought them off with the point of his bayonet but, at last, he drew concentrated rifle fire, was hit repeatedly and fell dead.

Simkins's men never faltered. So fierce was their resistance that they forced their enemy to retire. The engagement had begun and ended in so short a time that Simkins never summoned the main force. Shaw watched proudly as his men returned from their first fight, bringing news of their success. Nineteen-year-old Captain Cabot Russel, a small man whose life had been saved by a sergeant in his company, struggled back supporting a large wounded soldier. Another man walked alone, though his arm had been shattered and his sleeve was soaked with blood. Simkins came in last. His trousers and rubber coat had been ventilated by a rain of bullets, none of which had touched his flesh.

The resistance of the infantry and the support of the brigade's artillery were so persistent that the Confederates never mounted an attack in force. A war correspondent for *The Reflector* wrote

Peter Vogelsang in the uniform of a second lieutenant. Vogelsang was the oldest soldier in the Fifty Fourth. First a sergeant, he fought bravely on James Island, at Fort Wagner and elsewhere. He was commissioned in 1865. (Massachusetts Historical Society)

of the action of the Fifty Fourth, "The boys of the Tenth Connecticut could not help loving the men who saved them from destruction. . . . probably a thousand homes from Windham to Fairfield have in letters been told the story how the dark-skinned heroes fought the good fight and covered with their own brave hearts the retreat of brothers, sons and fathers of Connecticut."

After the successful action on James Island on July 16, the Fifty Fourth began an all-night march, in driving rain across a swamp, to reach their next objective. At 5:00 A.M., the regiment reached the beach opposite the southern tip of Folley Island and waited there for transport to Morris Island.

It was here that Shaw wrote his final letter to his wife. In this last letter, he wrote, "We have at last fought alongside white troops. Two hundred of my men on picket this morning were attacked by five regiments of infantry, some cavalry, and a battery of artillery." He wrote proudly, "I know this letter will give you pleasure, because what we have done today wipes out the remembrance of the Darien affair, which you could not but grieve over, though we were innocent participators." In a postscript, Shaw told his wife about the regiment's lack of food.

> I have had nothing but crackers and coffee these two days.
> It seems like old times in the army of the Potomac.
>
> Goodbye again, darling Annie.
> Rob.

At dawn on the morning of July 18, after a short voyage, the men of the Fifty Fourth arrived on Morris Island where they huddled in their tents, waiting to attack Fort Wagner. Some slept fitfully while others lay awake, thinking of the coming battle.

Shaw must have been reassured by the nearby thunder of the cannon of the Union siege line and the distant sound of the guns of the U.S. Navy squadron, standing offshore in the mist, but he had written his last letter and we can only guess what he was thinking. We do know that, on his final day, he entertained no shadow of a doubt about the justice of his cause, even though he must have understood that, for him, the path of glory almost certainly would lead to death.

7

THE OLD FLAG NEVER TOUCHED
THE GROUND
July 18, 1863–September 28, 1864

On the evening of July 18, Shaw approached Fort Wagner, crossed the moat and scrambled up the rampart. He was followed closely by the man who clung to the Massachusetts flag. Sergeant Carney took the stars and stripes up the slope, catching up to his commander, and with Shaw in the lead the three men advanced to the parapet, where Shaw's voice rang out, urging others to come forward. He stood, a silhouette against the smoke and flame, his sword pointing upward, then pitched forward and lay still.

After Shaw was shot and killed, the remnants of his regiment charged up the slope, toward the place where he had fallen, while scores of Confederate riflemen fired on them. Sergeant Carney, holding fast to the pole that held the stars and stripes, drove it hard into the sandy soil between two palmetto logs and crouched on the parapet, near the bodies of his fallen leader and the man who had carried the state flag, which by then was in tatters. There Carney, loading, firing and reloading an abandoned Enfield rifle, fought off his attackers.

The wounded and the dead tumbled headlong down the slope, most of them landing in the moat, where some who were still alive drowned in the salty waters. Sergeant Swails—a mature good looking man—remembered later that, in the pulsing light of cannon fire, he saw 19-year-old Captain Russel crumple near the bottom of the earthwork. Simkins, who was fond of Russel, paused to ask if he wanted him to call a stretcher-bearer. Russel shook his head but said he wanted to be straightened out. Simkins asked Swails to help him do this. Swails remembered that Simkins, ". . . while kneeling over his friend's head, facing the enemy, was himself hit. Putting his hand to his breast, he fell down from Russel, and never spoke or moved again."

Several more companies gained the rampart. Some of the attackers, standing on the crest, fired at gunners, keeping them from serving their field pieces. Others, entering the fort, attacked their enemy with bayonets and rifle butts. Some of the Confederate gunners joined the fray, using handspikes and gun-rammers. Sergeant Simmons leaped down from the parapet, engaged half a dozen riflemen in hand-to-hand combat and was wounded. Some men died where they stood while others, like Simmons, were surrounded, disarmed and taken prisoner. Hallowell reported later that the fight raged on the slope, on the parapet and in the fort, ". . . for about an hour."

As he led a company of men in the attack, Hallowell was wounded in the groin and forced to retreat. Captain Appleton—first to be commissioned in the regiment and first to begin recruiting, advanced straight toward the mouth of a cannon, crawled into its embrasure and directed pistol-fire at the men who served the gun. A private soldier of the Fifty Fourth, badly wounded in one arm, lay on his back and, with one hand, fed ammunition to a junior officer, enabling him to fire repeatedly at the Confederates in the fort. Several of Shaw's men remembered a Confederate sharpshooter, standing naked to the waist, dealing death, until he was targeted by three of Shaw's riflemen.

Sergeant Major Lewis Douglass, calling out in a voice that must have echoed that of his great father, rallied men who were unnerved by the slaughter, urging them to form a line. All his senior officers having been killed or wounded, Emilio assumed command. By now it was clear that the fort could not be taken by direct assault, but Emilio stood firm because he thought that the Confederates might attempt a counterattack. Later, in a letter to Emilio, Sergeant George E. Stephens gave his account of this portion of the action. "When we reached the Gatling battery drawn up to repel a counterattack, I remember you were the only commissioned officer present, and you placed us indiscriminately—that is, without regard to companies in line—and proposed to renew the charge. The commanding officer, whom I do not know, ordered us to the flanking rifle-pits, and we then awaited the expected counter-charge the enemy did not make."

A photograph of a reenactment of the storming of Fort Wagner staged during the filming of the motion picture Glory. (Courtesy TriStar Pictures, Inc.)

Emilio remembered that, "The charge of the Fifty Fourth had been made and repulsed before the arrival of any other troops."

By this time, it was clear to Sergeant Carney that retreat would soon be necessary. He knew that, in the darkness and the smoke, the flag he was defending had become invisible from below, so he grasped the pole once again and made his way down the slope, still under concentrated rifle fire from the southwest bastion. It was as dangerous to retire as to advance but Carney, already shot at least twice, bore the flag down the slope and gave it to Emilio. He might have waited for a stretcher bearer, but he made his way alone toward the distant field hospital.

There was no lack of courage or resolve among the commanders of supporting columns. Emilio blamed the lack of immediate support on the indecisive leadership of General Seymour, in command of the assault.

> Although the supports did not move forward with a close formation and promptness in support of the Fifty Fourth, which might have won Wagner that night, their attacks when made were delivered with a gallantry and persistence that made their severe losses the more deplorable and fruitless, by reason of such faulty generalship.

General Strong came forward with the leading elements of his brigade, dashing into undiminished cannon fire. He was severely wounded but lived long enough to testify to the extraordinary bravery of the Fifty Fourth. If Shaw's death had slowed the vanguard, the fall of Strong came close to stopping the advance of the supporting columns, a support that, because it came too late, accomplished little. Strong said later,

> The greatest number of men in the salient at any time hardly equalled a regiment, and were different organizations. They were fighting in a place unknown to them, holding their ground and repelling attacks, but were incapable of aggressive action. Fighting over traverses and sand-bags, hemmed in by a fire poured across their rear, as well as from the front and flanks, the struggle went on pitilessly for nearly two hours. Vainly were precious lives offered up, in heroic attempts to encourage a charge on the flanking guns. The enveloping darkness covered all; and the valiant, seeing how hopeless were their efforts, felt like crying. . . , "Give us light, O Jove! and in the light, if thou seest fit, destroy us!"

General Haldimand S. Putnam, who had argued that the fort could not be taken by direct assault, nonetheless followed orders and led a third wave of attackers into what had become a wasteland of dead and broken men. Before he passed the southeast bastion, Putnam was shot through the head. In the dark, as his men began to falter and were forced to retreat, elements of the One Hundredth New York Regiment mistook them for Confederate soldiers and began to fire on them, killing many.

Thereafter, two additional brigades—one commanded by Colonel Montgomery—were ordered to attack but fell back as they were swept up in what soon became a mass retreat. Emilio led what was left of his broken regiment back to the safety of the dunes. The Confederates had indeed contemplated a counterattack but there was little to be gained from taking ground that could be retaken easily and the fierceness of the Fifty Fourth's attack had convinced them to remain inside the fort.

Other Yankees heaped injustice on disaster. Emilio described the final horror of the night.

Upon the beach in front of the siege line, drunken soldiers of the regular artillery, with swords and pistol shots, barred the passage of all to the rear. They would listen to no protestations that the regiments were driven back or broken up, and even brutally ordered wounded men to the front. After a time, their muddled senses came to them on seeing the host of arrivals, while the vigorous actions of a few determined officers, who were prepared to enforce a free passage, made further opposition perilous.

Despite wounds in his chest and both arms and legs, Sergeant Carney, still alone, approached the field hospital—a large tent set up the day before and lit that night by the feeble yellow flames of lamps and candles. As he stumbled into the hospital, several of his comrades recognized him, raised themselves up from their cots and gave him a rousing cheer. He was reported to have said, "The dear old flag never touched the ground, boys!"

Following the demonstration of his bravery at Fort Wagner, Carney was awarded the Congressional Medal of Honor, becoming the first black man to be so recognized.

At midnight, Edward Pierce, who had watched the battle from a sand hill, rode across the battlefield.

The battle is over; it is midnight; the ocean beach is crowded with the dead, the dying and the wounded. It is with difficulty that you can urge your horse through to Lighthouse Inlet. Faint lights glimmer in the sand-holes and rifle pits where many a poor bleeding soldier has lain down to his last sleep.

That night, rescuers braved sporadic rifle fire to crawl among the dead and wounded, listening for signs of life, and dragged the wounded to the cover of a dune where the stretcher bearers waited.

The pink light of a Sunday dawn touched the dunes and pine barrens lying between Fort Wagner and Fort Johnson—on the eastern tip of James Island. The rim of the sun appeared where the ocean met the sky and, above the placid harbor, shone the spires of Charleston's churches, first to catch the early light. No doubt, by now, most of the city's citizens had heard the news spelled out in a telegram sent to his superiors by General Beauregard, who had been in command of the defending forces. "PRAISE BE TO GOD. ANNIVERSARY OF BULL RUN GLORI-

OUSLY CELEBRATED." Beauregard, who was referring to the first battle of Bull Run, had his dates wrong, but no doubt his commanders took his sentiments to heart.

The beach, the moat and the slopes of the work were littered with the corpses of young men who, 12 hours earlier, had been living breathing soldiers, men who had left their families to go off to war. Blacks and whites lay together, strewn across three quarters of a mile of sand. There were perhaps 100 bodies in the moat—soldiers deaf to the eternal dirge of the great ocean that, in time, was to lay claim to their bones.

Praise for the bravery of the Fifty Fourth came from almost every quarter. A Confederate officer—Lieutenant Iredell Jones—toured the field. Later he remembered,

> One pile of negroes numbered thirty. Numbers of both white and black were killed on top of our breastworks as well as inside. The negroes fought gallantly, and were headed by as brave a colonel as ever lived. He mounted the breastworks waving his sword, and at the head of his regiment, and he and a negro orderly sergeant fell dead over the inner crest of the works. The negroes were as fine-looking a set as I ever saw—large, strong muscular fellows.

Corporal James Gooding, not mentioned in Emilio's account of the storming of the fort, sent letters to his home-town paper—*The New Bedford Mercury*—and, in one, gave an account of the attack, in which he stated that, before Shaw was hit, Shaw seized the staff that held the state colors. This account is contradicted by Stephens who wrote,

> Col. Shaw, our noble and lamented commander, was the bravest of the brave. He . . . led the column up to the fort, and was the first man who stood up on the parapet of the fort. When, he reached it he said, 'Come on, follow me!' and he either received a mortal wound or fell over the wall, or stumbled in[to] the fort and was killed.

To his report, Gooding added, "When the men saw their gallant leader fall, they made a desperate effort to get him out, but they were either shot down or reeled in [to] the ditch below."

Though he was badly wounded, Strong talked to a reporter for the New York *Evening Post*. He said that, following two nights

Drummer-boy Henry A. Monroe, from New Bedford, Massachusetts, was listed as 18 but was probably much younger. Many boys lied about their ages so that they could go to war, on one side or the other. (Massachusetts Historical Society)

with very little sleep and a day without food, the regiment had, ". . . stormed the fort, faced a stream of fire, faltered not till the ranks were broken by shot and shell; and in all these severe tests, which would have tried even veteran troops, they fully met my expectations. . . ."

John T. Luck, a U.S. Navy surgeon attached to the gunboat *Pawnee,* was taken prisoner while caring for the wounded. Luck was shown the body of a man in a colonel's uniform and that of the sergeant who had fallen with him. The colonel was identified as Shaw. Luck was told to move along and was compelled to leave Shaw's body to its fate.

Years later, a Confederate officer, who seems to have had no ax to grind, wrote, "The morning following the battle his body was carried through our lines; and I noticed that he was stripped of all his clothing save under-vest and drawers. This desecration of the dead we endeavored to provide against but . . . our men were so frenzied that it was next to impossible to guard against."

All agree that Shaw was buried in a common trench with his enlisted men and that his white officers were buried in a separate place. There is ample evidence that this was done deliberately, as an affront to the memory of a man who had dared to lead black men into battle. Confederate General Hagood—who took command from Taliaferro on the morning of July 19—was reported to have said, "I shall bury him in the common trench with the negroes that fell with him." A more colorful outburst was credited to Hagood, which was repeated often in the North. "He is buried with his niggers."

The vivid and dynamic George Stearns responded quickly to the news of the attack on Fort Wagner. Writing of the bravery of the Fifty Fourth, he said,

> I feel that they are my children whom I induced to rush into the jaws of death. Many of the names of privates wounded are familiar to me and I can recall many of their faces. I should sometimes be tempted to say, "Oh Lord how long?" did I not clearly see that this baptism of fire was necessary for the regeneration of both races.

As soon as possible, the severely wounded were removed to military hospitals in Beaufort. In the hospital for enlisted men, Charlotte Forten went to work with the surgeons and the nurses. She liked the large brick house, which overlooked the water and was ". . . in every way well adapted for a hospital." On July 20, she wrote in her diary,

> Tonight comes news, oh, so sad, so heart sickening. It is too terrible, too terrible to write. We can only hope that it

may not all be true. That our noble, beautiful young
Colonel is killed, and the regiment cut to pieces! I cannot,
cannot believe it. And yet I know that it may be so. But oh,
I am stunned, sick at heart. I can scarcely write. . . .
Thank Heaven! they fought bravely! And oh, I still must
hope that our colonel, *ours* especially he seems to me, is
not killed. But I can write no more tonight.

In Beaufort, writing letters for the wounded, she noted, "It
was pleasant to see the brave, cheerful, uncomplaining spirit
which they all breathed." A rumor circulated that Shaw had
been wounded but was still alive.

How joyfully their wan faces lighted up! They almost
started from their couches. . . . Brave and grateful hearts!
I hope they will ever prove worthy of such a leader. And
God grant that he may indeed be living. But I fear, I greatly
fear that it may be a false report.

On July 24, Shaw's death was at last confirmed. Forten wrote,

I know it was a glorious death. But oh, it is hard, very hard
for the young wife so late a bride, for the invalid mother,
whose only and most dearly loved son he was, that heroic
mother who rejoiced in the position which he occupied as
colonel of a colored regiment. My heart bleeds for her.

When Forten went to visit Hallowell, he spoke of Shaw
with great respect and tenderness, then told her about
Shaw's wish that, if he fell, she be given one of his three
horses. She wrote, "I shall treasure this gift most sacredly,
all my life long."

In Beaufort, General Strong was growing weaker every day
but found the strength to write a note to Shaw's parents, in
which he expressed his affection and respect for his subordi-
nate. A day or so before he died, Strong spoke to Edward
Pierce about the Fifty Fourth. Pierce wrote Governor Andrew,

I asked General Strong if he had any testimony in relation
to the regiment to be communicated to you. These are his
precise words, "The Fifty Fourth did well and nobly; only
the fall of Colonel Shaw prevented them from entering the

fort. They moved up as gallantly as any troops could, and with their enthusiasm they deserved a better fate."

Sergeant Simmons was sent to Charleston, with some 60 other prisoners, 20 of whom had been wounded. Emilio reported later, "First Sergeant Simmons of Company B was the finest-looking soldier in the Fifty Fourth—a brave man and of good education. He was wounded and captured. Taken to Charleston, his bearing impressed even his captors." Simmons had been wounded in an arm. He languished in a Charleston jail until his wound became infected. In great pain, he was removed to the Old Marine Hospital. There his arm was amputated. There he died.

Of the 60 who remained in Charleston, two men had been slaves. The Confederate Congress had declared such men outlaws, to be tried in the courts of the states where they were taken. Here was a chance for South Carolina to make good the promise of harsh treatment for escaped slaves who had fought against the Confederate forces. In order to protect these men and others who might follow, Lincoln issued the following proclamation:

EXECUTIVE MANSION, Washington, July 30, 1863

It is the duty of every government to give protection to its citizens of whatever class, color, or condition, and especially to those who are duly organized as soldiers in the public service. The law of nations and the usages and customs of war, as carried on by civilized powers, permit no distinction as to color in the treatment of prisoners of war as public enemies. To sell or enslave any captured person on account of his color, and for no offense against the laws of war, is a relapse into barbarism and a crime against the civilization of the age. The Government of the United States will give the same protection to all its soldiers; and if the enemy shall sell or enslave any one because of his color, the offense shall be punished by retaliation upon the enemy's prisoners in our hands.

It is therefore ordered that for every soldier of the United States killed in violation of the laws of war, a Rebel soldier shall be executed, and for every one enslaved by the enemy or sold into slavery, a Rebel soldier shall be placed at hard labor on the public works, and continue such labor until the other shall be released and receive the treatment due a prisoner of war.

Abraham Lincoln.
By order of the Secretary of War,
E. D. Townsend, *Assistant*
Adjutant General.

Despite Lincoln's edict, South Carolina's Governor Milledge Luke Bonham demanded that the two men who had been slaves be tried in a South Carolina court. Charleston harbored a few people who were loyal to the Union. One of these was attorney Nelson Mitchell who, though he could ill afford to do so, took it upon himself to defend former slaves Sergeant Walter Jeffries and Corporal Charles Hardy. Though Mitchell understood the broad implications of the case, he won it on the grounds that the two men had not been South Carolina slaves. Lincoln's threat of retaliation against those who meted out unfair treatment to black soldiers captured in combat must have had its effect. Though Governor Bonham said he wasn't pleased with the finding of his court, he may have helped bring it about. Confederate President Jefferson Davis was reluctant to take action against captured black men, feeling that the whole question was, ". . . fraught with present difficulty and future danger." And, close to home, Bonham had a stake in the fate of the black soldiers. His cousin Sallie Butler wrote to him from Greenville, asking him to stay his hand.

> I have been asked by a member of Campbell Williams' family to write and beg you to spare these negroes on *his* account. He is a prisoner in the hands of the Yankees, & has been selected to be *hung* in retaliation for those negroes which we have taken. This poor mother has just lost a noble son in the battle of Brandy Station & now this son is to be hung. We heard the matter had been left entirely in your hands. . . . Mrs. Williams is a widow & in affliction at this time. He is so *young* and so dear to his family.

Williams was not hung.

Jeffries and Hardy were returned to jail, where they stayed until they were released in the spring of 1865. While rich and aristocratic

Charleston Unionists were tolerated by their fellow townsmen, Nelson Mitchell was roundly scorned and died in poverty.

While Lincoln's proclamation may have had some effect in the case of Jeffries and Hardy, its impact was limited. On April 12, 1864, black soldiers captured at Fort Pillow, an outpost on the Mississippi, were killed after they surrendered. A black private who was shot but survived, gave extraordinary testimony.

> "Who shot you?"
> "A rebel soldier."
> "How near did he come to you?"
> "About ten feet."
> "What did he say to you?"
> "He said, 'Damn you, what are you doing here?' I said, 'Please don't shoot me.' He said, 'Damn you, you are fighting against your master.' He raised his gun and fired, and the bullet went into my mouth and out the back part of my head. They threw me into the river, and I swam around and hung on there in the water until night."

The same man testified that boys not more than 16 years old, who weren't soldiers but had worked as laborers, were shot dead. Nor were all these killings done directly after battle. Some were done in cold blood a day later. After this massacre, Confederate soldiers often heard the battle cry, "Remember Fort Pillow!"

Following their attack on Fort Wagner, the soldiers of the Fifty Fourth served out the war in coastal regions of the South. No story of the regiment would be complete if it did not include at least a brief account of its activities through 1865.

After the retreat from Fort Wagner, some 400 soldiers of the regiment remained in camp on the southern tip of Morris Island. These included men with wounds that could be treated in the field. The men who had remained on St. Helena rejoined the regiment and, for awhile, Captain Emilo retained command.

Union generals had begun to realize that it was all but useless to attack entrenched Confederates—men who were fighting to defend their own country, their own land. Such attacks had failed repeatedly in the West and in the East and it became apparent that strongholds, like Fort Wagner, would yield only to persistent siege.

Captain Luis F. Emilio took command of the Fifty Fourth after Shaw was killed and Hallowell was wounded at Fort Wagner. Emilio performed heroically in pressing the attack and in organizing the withdrawal. He survived the war and wrote a history of the regiment, which was published first in 1891. (Massachusetts Historical Society)

On Morris Island, Union artillery remained in place and additional heavy weapons were brought in and positioned on the island. On August 17, 1863, the land batteries joined the navy in bombarding Fort Wagner and Fort Sumter. General Beauregard, still commanding the defenses around Charleston, refused to yield to threats that the city would be fired on and, on August 22, in the early morning hours, the guns of a battery situated in a marsh between Morris and James Islands opened fire on the tip of the peninsula where the windows of the city's stately houses faced the harbor and the sea. The main element of this extraordinary battery—called Swamp Angel—was a huge Parrott gun whose barrel burst after the first few discharges but other guns were used to continue the bombardment.

During the positioning of guns and the siege of Fort Wagner, the soldiers of the Fifty Fourth were used as laborers. It must be said that Union soldiers, black and white, in all theaters of the Civil War, were often used as laborers. Fighting took up very little time in the life of any soldier and, though the South had thousands of slave laborers, the North did not and so used its fighting men. In his regimental history, Emilio wrote about the appearance of his soldiers after weeks of fatigue duty. "Clothes were in rags, shoes worn out, and haversacks full of holes."

The last Confederate soldier left Fort Wagner 58 days after the siege began. Shaw's friend Ned Hallowell—by then recovered from his wound and promoted to the rank of colonel—took Shaw's place as the commander of the Fifty Fourth. He was present and presiding when the stars and stripes were raised above the ruins of the fort.

As late as December, Fort Sumter was still occupied by the Confederates and the ships of the blockading squadron hadn't dared steam through the channel to take Charleston. In fact, though it suffered the destruction of many of its buildings, Charleston never would become a battleground.

In 1864, at the end of January, the Fifty Fourth joined an expedition to the Florida mainland, as part of an effort to extend the blockade of Southern ports and act in response to Lincoln's notion that the state of Florida—which had seceded in 1861—might rejoin the Union under pressure. During this expedition, an attempt to drive back Confederate forces west of Jacksonville led to the Battle of Olustee, or Ocean Pond, which took place on February 20.

In the bloody battle of Olustee, it was demonstrated once again that episodic raids on the mainland, even ones involving 20,000 soldiers, had little chance of success. In a letter to a friend, one of Hallowell's young officers told the story of the part played by the Fifty Fourth in the battle. He wrote that the regiment was sent in when the battle was already lost. He quoted General Seymour, who spoke unsparingly to Hallowell. "The day is lost. You must go in and save the corps."

The young officer continued, "We did go in and did save it, checked the enemy, held the field, and were the last to leave—and covered the retreat." In summing up, he wrote bluntly, "We have had a fight, a licking, and a foot-race. We marched 110 miles in 108 hours, and in that time had a three hour's fight. Our regiment lost one man in every five—going in five hundred strong, and losing one hundred in killed, wounded, and missing. . . . When we returned to Jacksonville we were all crippled from severe marching."

Late in 1864, the Fifty Fourth took part in another expedition to the mainland. In Port Royal, the regiment was organized as part of what was called the Coast Division, under General John P. Hatch who was ordered to cut the Charleston and Savannah Railroad at Pocotaligo, South Carolina.

Advancing toward Pocotaligo, a white regiment was stopped at an earthwork and pinned down by heavy fire. Moving forward in support of the white regiment, the Fifty Fourth, by then famous, was roundly hailed, but the assault on the Confederate work, which was positioned on high ground and reinforced, was doomed to fail.

Heroes in battle, the men of the Fifty Fourth became heroes in retreat. Emilio wrote about the removal of the wounded. "Stretchers were improvised from muskets, shelter tents and blankets, by which means and bodily help, the Fifty Fourth alone carried one hundred and fifty wounded from the field. When we came to Bolan's church, the whole vicinity was weirdly lighted by great fires of fence rails and brushwood. A confused turmoil of sounds pervaded the night air—the rumbling of artillery, the creaking of wagons of the train, and the shouts of drivers urging on their animals."

John Andrew, the father of the heroic Fifty Fourth, was himself a war hero. He gave all his energies to the war effort, especially to the realization of his belief that black Americans must fight for the freedom they held dear and, in so doing, must be treated with respect. At times, during the long fratricidal conflict, his friends were afraid that Andrew might not go the distance. One friend, who talked to him on Tremont Street,

Sergeant Henry Stewart—called Harry—was a barber from Horseheads, New York, who fought at Fort Wagner. (Massachusetts Historical Society)

thought he had a worn and haunted look, as if he anticipated death. In fact, he was to die in 1867.

Andrew, tired but insistent, kept on waging the fight for equal pay for soldiers in black regiments. Not one to forget a promise, he remembered his to Shaw. In his reply to Shaw's letter of July 2, he had written reassuringly of his faith in Edwin M. Stanton, "The Secretary of War will cause right to be done so soon as the case is presented to him and shall be fully understood."

Shaw died before Andrew's letter reached him. On August 5, the paymaster for the government in Washington informed the men of the Fifty Fourth that they could collect full pay, minus an allowance for the cost of clothing—a deduction never made from the pay of the soldiers of white regiments. Again, the Fifty Fourth refused short pay.

It was September before Andrew could leave Boston, go himself to Washington and plead his case. There, he talked to Lincoln and to Stanton, both of whom admitted that a promise had been made and should be kept.

So slow was the federal government in meeting its commitment, that Andrew offered to make up deficiencies from state funds. He was aware that it was possible for soldiers to survive without pay. After all, they were fed, clothed and armed at government expense, but he knew that the families of these men often suffered deprivation.

Hallowell thanked the governor but expressed the will of his officers and men when he declared that it was the responsibility of the federal government to pay its soldiers all the money that was due them from the day of their enlistment.

In December, an unidentified soldier of the Fifty Fourth voiced a common sentiment, "For four months we have been steadily working night and day under fire. And such work! Up to our knees in mud half the time, causing the tearing and wearing out of more than one volunteer's yearly allowance of clothing." The men were denied time to wash and repair their clothes, time to drill, time to bury their own dead. "All this we have borne patiently, waiting for justice."

Journalist Theodore Tilton said of the black soldiers,

> They are not willing that the Federal Government should throw mud upon them, even though Massachusetts stands ready to wipe it off. And perhaps it is not unsoldierly in a soldier, white or black, to object to being insulted by a government which he heroically serves. The regiment whose bayonets pricked the name of Colonel Shaw into the roll of immortal honor can afford to be cheated out of their money, but not out of their manhood.

Colonel James Montgomery directed threats at members of the Fifty Fourth, saying, "In refusing to take the pay offered you, and what you are only legally entitled to, you are guilty of insubordination and mutiny, and can be tried and shot by court-martial."

No member of the Fifty Fourth was shot, but Sergeant William Walker, member of a following black regiment, was tried and executed for refusing to do duty until he was paid what he was due. Walker was a good soldier, not a trouble-maker. He was not a mutineer but was a man reaching out for simple justice. Andrew, hearing of the case, expressed cold fury: "The Government which found no law to pay him except as a nondescript and a contraband, nevertheless found law enough to shoot him as a soldier."

Too late to right the many wrongs suffered by black soldiers and their families—not to mention the harm done to recruiting efforts—the government in Washington kept its promise and, on September 28, 1864, the men of the Fifty Fourth were paid all the money that was due them. An observer wrote,

> There was use in waiting! Two days have changed the face of things. . . . The fiddle and other music long neglected enlivens the tents day and night. Song burst out everywhere. Dancing is incessant, boisterous shouts are heard, mimicry, burlesque, and carnival. . . .

8

THE HIGH SOUL BURNS ON
1863–1897

On Staten Island, Shaw's parents heard the news of their son's death. Lydia Maria Child was among the first to write to Sarah Shaw. "Oh darling! Darling! if the newspaper rumour be true, what I have so long dreaded has come upon you. . . . If the report be true, may our Heavenly Father sustain you under this heavy sorrow." She continued, "Your darling Robert made the most of the powers and advantages God has given him, by consecrating them to the defense of freedom and humanity."

The manner of Shaw's burial was reported widely in the North. When Shaw's parents heard that efforts might be made to recover their son's body, they reacted swifty. Francis Shaw wrote General Gillmore, "We hold that a soldier's most appropriate burial-place is on the field where he has fallen. I shall be much obliged, General, if in case the matter is brought to your cognizance, you will forbid the desecration of my son's grave, and prevent the disturbance of his remains or those buried with him."

When William Lloyd Garrison saw a copy of the letter, he praised Francis Shaw. "Your letter to General Gillmore, concerning the removal of the body of Robert, thrilled my heart. . . . "

Young Henry James, brother of Adjutant Garth James, wrote Shaw's father,

> I feel for you and Mrs. Shaw and the girls, more than I can put in fitting words. . . . It is a great leaf in God's book of life, now fully turned over for you, and I cannot but believe that the lesson of it will be erelong altogether welcome. . . .

In the mystical Creation, we are told that "the evening and the morning were the first day" . . . This is because in Divine order all progress is from dark to bright, from evil to good, from low to high, and never contrariwise.

Morris Copeland wrote, "I saw the short telegraphic despatch, and as the awful fact stood clear before me, it seemed that God might have spared us this blow. . . . "
Charlotte Forten voiced a lament that has echoed through the ages. "It seems very, very hard that the best and noblest must be the earliest called away." Her work in the hospital— her immediate exposure to the tragedies of war—took its toll on the sensitive young teacher. Her health began to fail. Her doctor, Seth Rogers, who was also a good friend, was close by, serving with Higginson. He advised her to take a vacation in the North. Accordingly, she sailed with him, Edward Pierce and several other Yankees, aboard the steamer *Fulton,* to New York. In Philadelphia, she wrote to Shaw's mother of her son.

> The singular charm of his manner, the nobleness of soul that shone through his face, won all hearts to him. And it is not strange that I, belonging to the unhappy race for whom he gave his life, should have a feeling of deep personal gratitude mingled with the affectionate admiration with which I, from the very first, regarded him.

Remembering her promise to write down the words of the songs she and Shaw had heard sung by people of the islands, she said,

> I was very glad to copy them for him, but had not quite finished them when the regiment was ordered away. I send them to you, thinking you might like to have them, as they were copied for him.

Then she wrote of the dedication of Shaw's wounded men to their commander.

> I believe there was not one who would not willingly have laid down his life for him. How warmly, how affectionately they spoke of him. "He was one of the very best men in the world," they said. "No one could be kinder to a set of men than he was to us."

She went on, "I think they will ever prove worthy of the gallant young leader. . . whom they loved so well, and who gave all for them."

Before she left her native city, Forten went to visit Edward Hallowell, who was still recuperating. "Found him much improved, sitting up and looking quite cheerful and happy." She added, "It seems as if one could not but get well in such a lovely place and with such tender care."

The next day, she left for Salem, Massachusetts, where she had been a student and a teacher. Shaw's father, aware of the short, intense friendship between her and his son, met her at a Boston railroad station. As might have been expected, Francis Shaw was grieving deeply. Certainly, he was proud of his son's accomplishment but took less comfort from his heroism than Shaw's mother seemed to take. Forten had another train to catch and her visit with Shaw's father was as short as her comment in her diary, "He has a noble face, but very sad."

Shaw's wife, Annie Haggerty, was as devoted to Shaw's memory as she had been to the young soldier and his cause. It is hard to reconstruct their courtship and their pitifully brief marriage, which produced no children. She asked that all her letters to him be destroyed. Shaw promised to destroy them and he did. Certainly, they loved each other. Restrained though they often are, Shaw's letters tell us that.

Annie Shaw was a private person but, nine months after Shaw's death, when enlistment in black regiments was becoming commonplace, she watched while New York's first black regiment passed in review. She was proud because she knew that her husband had helped pave the way for recruitment of this regiment and the many that would follow. The people of the city where, less than a year before, three days of rioting had terrified black citizens and where some had lost their lives, cheered wildly as the Twentieth Regiment United States Colored Troops went off to war.

Annie Shaw never chose to remarry. She lived in France and Switzerland for a while, then went home to Boston, where she died many years later in her sister's house on Commonwealth Avenue. She had asked that she be laid to rest in a country churchyard in Lenox, Massachusetts—a village where many members of her family lived and where she had spent her honeymoon.

The New Englander who carved Annie Shaw's tombstone must have been told to celebrate her Irish heritage. The stone—which in spring is surrounded by small daisies—is topped by a simple Celtic cross. It bears the legend, "Sacred to the memory of Anna Kneeland Haggerty, Widow of Colonel Robert Gould Shaw." The lettering below this tells us she was born on July 9, 1835 and that she died on March 17, 1907. On the back of the stone, which faces toward the setting sun, are the initials A.K.S., above the words, "Behold we count them happy which endure."

Shaw had told his young wife that the bravery of the Fifty Fourth on James Island, ". . . wipes out the memory of the Darien affair." It did not. In fact, in many quarters, Shaw himself was blamed for the barbaric action. In 1959, historian Merton Coulter wrote a definitive account of the raid, in which he showed that it was James Montgomery who must bear responsibility for the burning of the town. Montgomery's raid on Darien caused enduring bitterness in the South. General Beauregard blamed the raid on the commanders of the expedition and on, ". . . the employment of a merciless, servile race as soldiers."

The parishioners of St. Andrew's Episcopal Church, in Darien, which was burnt to the ground, could not afford to rebuild, and wealthy planters, including Pierce Butler, contributed to a fund to build a chapel on a ridge near the town. Fund-raisers published an appeal in *Harper's Weekly,* in which they stated that Shaw was responsible for the firing of the town. Shaw's mother, still grieving over her son's forced connection to the raid, saw the appeal and wrote to set the record straight. She received a gracious answer and replied in part, "Had you known our son, you would understand why all his friends hastened to shield his memory. He died after 25 years of a fine and lovely life and left only sweet memories behind." Shaw's parents sent two generous checks to help in the construction of the chapel. These were followed by other, lesser, checks from other members of Shaw's family and his friends. As Darien itself rose from its ashes, new churches went up on new sites. One of these was a replacement for the first St. Andrew's. Construction of the new St. Andrew's was begun in 1876 and completed in 1879.

There is no monument to Shaw on Morris Island, where he died. The soldiers of the Fifty Fourth, together with contrabands who lived on St. Helena, in Beaufort and elsewhere, gave money they could ill-afford for the raising of a monument on or near the remains of Fort Wagner but the shifting sands of an Atlantic beach seemed a poor site.

There is a modest stone in a churchyard close to where Shaw's family lived on Staten Island. This monument is maintained by some of his and his wife's relatives and by others loyal to his memory.

Shortly after Shaw's death, Andrew appointed a committee to plan and erect a fitting monument in Boston. The committee's chairman was John Murray Forbes; perhaps its most enthusiastic member was Joshua Smith, who had once been a fugitive from slavery, had been a servant in the house on Bowdoin Street where Shaw had spent his early childhood and was a successful caterer.

When he called for money to support the project, Andrew said,

> The monument is intended not only to mark the public gratitude to the fallen hero, who at a critical moment assumed perilous responsibility, but also to commemorate that event wherein he was a leader, by which title of colored men as citizen soldiers was fixed beyond recall.

At first, Shaw's parents, who believed that their son's deeds were monument enough, failed to give the project their unqualified support, saying only that any monument so raised must bear the names of everyone who fell in the July 18 attack. Perhaps because of this, things remained unsettled for almost 20 years. Several sculptors were considered and abandoned or rejected.

Then Augustus Saint-Gaudens, a young sculptor who was gaining prominence, came to the attention of Forbes and those committee members who were still alive and active.

In 1861, when Shaw had marched in New York's Seventh Regiment from Tompkins Market to the ferry that would take him to the New Jersey Railroad Depot, Saint-Gaudens was 13 and working in New York as an apprentice to a jeweler. Sitting at his workbench, he heard the tumult as Shaw's regiment passed in review but probably saw no more than the tips of burnished bayonets above the heads of the onlookers. By the

Head of an anonymous black soldier, a sculpture done by Saint-Gaudens as a preliminary study for his monument to Shaw and the men who fought and died with him. Saint-Gaudens did many such rough studies for the memorial. He noted, "I modelled about forty heads of which I selected the sixteen that are visible in the relief. Some heads that were very good I rejected. . . . " (Photograph by Richard Benson)

time Saint-Gaudens drew his first sketch for the monument to Shaw, he had studied sculpture, not only in New York, but in Rome and Paris, and had demonstrated his great talent. However, Shaw's parents didn't like the sketch, which showed their son alone, mounted and bareheaded. The sculptor's second sketch, which depicted Shaw mounted but beside his men, as he had been on May 28, 1863, on his march down Beacon Street, pleased them. Saint-Gaudens then began what turned out to be his greatest work.

Detail from the Saint-Gaudens monument. (The Houghton Library, Harvard University)

Two years were allotted for the project but Saint-Gaudens wouldn't let himself be hurried. Two years became four, then eight. He worked on. At the time, he made no excuses but much later he explained, "My own delay, I excuse on the grounds that a sculptor's work endures for so long that it is next to a crime for him to neglect to do everything that lies in his power to execute a result that will not be a disgrace. . . . "

The statue was at last unveiled on May 31, 1897, a gray day that brought light rain. Leaders of both races waited on the crest of Beacon Hill, to deliver their orations but what most impressed Saint-Gaudens was the appearance of a column of black veterans who marched proudly up the hill to do honor to their fallen comrades.

Eight years later, Saint-Gaudens remembered, "The impression of those old soldiers passing the very spot where they left for the war so many years before, thrills me even as I write these words. They seemed as if returning from the war. . . . It was a consecration."

At the dedication of the monument, Shaw was praised. His men were commended. Philosopher William James, who gave the longest speech of the day, said,

> Look at that monument and read the story—see the mingling of elements which the sculptor's genius has brought so vividly before the eye. There on foot go the dark outcasts, so true to nature that one can almost hear them breathing as they march. State after State by its laws had denied them to be human persons. The Southern leaders in congressional debates, insolent in their security of legalized possession, loved most to designate them by the contemptuous collective epithet of "this peculiar kind of property." There they march, warm blooded champions of a better day for man. There on horseback, among them, in his very habit as he lived, sits the blue-eyed child of fortune, upon whose happy youth every divinity had smiled. Onward they move together, a single resolution kindled in their

Detail from the Saint-Gaudens monument. (The Houghton Library, Harvard University)

> eyes, and animating their otherwise so different frames.
> The bronze that makes their memory eternal betrays the
> very soul and secret of those awful years.

In his speech, James failed to say exactly what he thought and felt. Five days later, in a letter to his brother Henry, he wrote, ". . . everything softened and made unreal by distance, poor little Robert Shaw erected into a great symbol of deeper things than he ever realized himself."

The truth about Shaw lies somewhere between the myth of the young man born in a bright city on a hill, who willingly went to his death to free a race despised, and the vision of a boy who became his mother's sacrificial lamb. The truth is more inspiring, more important, than the myth.

Frederick Douglass had died two years earlier but another leader of his people, educator Booker T. Washington, spoke in his stead. Denounced widely as conservative, Washington was, above all, a peacemaker. He talked about what the monument stood for, then said, "What these heroic souls of the 54th Regiment began, we must complete." He continued, "Standing as I do to-day in the home of Garrison and Phillips and Sumner, my heart goes out to those who wore the gray as well as those clothed in blue. . . . "

Like Shaw, Washington was small of stature. He must have risen to his full height as he said, "If through me, an humble representative, nearly ten millions of my people might be permitted to send a message to Massachusetts, to the survivors of the 54th Regiment. . . to the family who gave their only boy that we might have life more abundantly, that message would be: Tell them that the sacrifice was not in vain, that up from the depths of ignorance and poverty we are coming. . . . by way of the school, the well-cultivated field, the skilled hand. . . . we are coming up. . . . "

Shaw's bravery was extraordinary, but the glory of his life can be found in his capacity to love, and so to grow. In the end, as he walked among his men, expressing his affection for them, it was clear that had risen above prejudice, above his mother's single-minded devotion to her cause, above demands made on him by his elevated social status. In the end he was a man who understood that he walked among his equals and he knew that he and those who marched with him must demonstrate their unshakable conviction that black men and women would, soon, take their rightful places as citizens of a great democracy.

AFTERWORD

Following the Battle of Gettysburg, Lee retreated to the banks of the Potomac, as he had done after his withdrawal from Sharpsburg. This time, there were differences. As his immense wagon train of wounded and exhausted men jolted over rutted roads and approached the river, he saw that raiders had destroyed his pontoon bridge and that the waters were so high as to prevent a fording of the stream.

Lincoln had dismissed McClellan shortly after Antietam and Union forces—this time under General George G. Meade—failed again to pursue their enemy. A week later, Lee escaped.

While the slaughter in Pennsylvania was in progress, General Grant captured Vicksburg, Mississippi. Grant's successes in the West made him conspicuous and, in time, Lincoln was to call on him to take command of all the armies—East and West—and direct military operations in the East.

The Confederacy was in trouble economically and was made to rely on a weakened military force. Moreover, with Grant's arrival in the East, Lee would have to face a determined and aggressive general, a man who favored the enlistment of black soldiers in his army. Grant had recognized the value of black soldiers who had served in his command in the West and had heard of their courage in the South—above all of the bravery of the Fifty Fourth Massachusetts Regiment. In a letter to Lincoln, written on August 23, 1863, Grant left no doubt about his views. "I have given the subject of arming the negro my hearty support. This, with the emancipation of the negro, is the heaviest blow yet given the Confederacy. . . . By arming the negro we have added a powerful ally."

In a public letter published three days later, Lincoln spoke directly to white Union soldiers, many of whom harbored bitterness against black Americans. "You say you will not fight to free negroes. Some of them seem willing to fight for you. . . . There will be some black men who can remember that, with silent tongue, and clenched teeth, and steady eye, and well-poised bayonet, they have helped mankind on to this great consummation; while, I fear, there will be some white ones, unable to forget that, with malignant heart, and deceitful speech, they have strove to hinder it."

When Grant went East, General William Tecumseh Sherman took command in the West. Sherman is an interesting study. His sweeping operations in the West and in the South—together with Grant's performance in the East—spelled the doom of the Confederacy but, though he expressed great kindness toward the slaves he liberated, nothing would persuade him to employ black fighting men in his army.

Sherman's Atlanta campaign began in the spring of 1864. In the cruelest and the most effective operation of the war, Sherman took 100,000 men—including cavalry—on a bold march along the railroad line from Chattanooga to Atlanta. On his way, he repeatedly outflanked his defenders.

At last, early in July, he crossed the Chattahoochee River, northwest of Atlanta, and the men in his command dug in around the city. There, he concentrated on encirclement, sending forces to his right, where they severed railroad lines coming in from the south and the southwest.

As complete encirclement became a certainty, General John B. Hood, who commanded the defending forces, made plans to retreat and, on September 1, after dark, the sky lit up and the ground shook as Hood's men blew up Confederate railroad cars filled with ammunition.

Two weeks later, Sherman told his commanders to give orders to incinerate the city. His troops took to the task with gusto, leaving most of it in ashes and, before the smoke had blown away, Sherman led his armies toward the sea.

Many people think of Sherman as a hard, relentless man, as a satanic figure who had no redeeming features, but his soldiers loved him. He was indeed relentless but he was also a cultivated man, widely known for his charm and honesty. He was an artist—an accomplished amateur. He often quoted from the poetry and plays of Shakespeare.

Sherman's attitude toward war was, if nothing else, consistent. He said, "To make war we must and will harden our hearts. . . . know that war, like the thunderbolt, follows its laws and turns not aside even if the beautiful, the virtuous and charitable stand in its path."

Why, then, did he not employ black troops? Certainly, he was not an abolitionist, nor it seems was he a pragmatist, as was Grant. In fact, he said bluntly, "I would prefer to have this a white man's war and provide for the negroes after the time has passed but we are in revolution and I must not pretend to judge. With my opinions of negroes and my experience, yea, prejudice, I cannot trust them yet."

There is sadness in most stories of triumph, as there is in the story of the victory over slavery in America. In waging the first modern warfare, Sherman used brutal tactics. It was not surprising, then, that there were black Southerners, as well as white ones, who were frightened of invading Union soldiers but, as Sherman and his legions passed, most slaves streamed away from their quarters, left the fields they knew so well and followed Sherman, as if he were a Moses, come to lead them to the promised land. They came with all their children, a variety of animals and their pathetic hordes of worldly goods and, when Sherman's columns were attacked by Confederates, those few who were armed or could borrow firearms, crawled behind their carts and wagons and helped to defend their savior and his men. These former slaves had no idea what lay in store for them. Sherman had set them free and, one way or another, freedom in itself would bring the dawn of a new day. Seeing that these people trusted him, Sherman was compassionate, but philosopher Ralph Waldo Emerson had it right when he said, "Liberty is a slow fruit."

As hundreds of refugees joined his march from Atlanta to Savannah, Sherman knew he couldn't feed them all. Outside the town of Covington, he singled out an elder—an old man with a head of snow white hair—and asked for his cooperation in unburdening an army that was living off the land. The man understood and spread the word and, after that, for awhile, only young men and women who could help the Yankees tagged along but, during the march to the sea, a great many fugitives came to see and talk to Sherman and, busy as he was, he found time to talk them. It was said that he spoke frankly, pleasantly, to them, that he put them at their ease and did not talk down to them.

It is a great irony that the Union general slaves most loved was a man who knew that slavery had brought war but who had never preached against the institution. It is strange that it was such a man who led a march the likes of which John Brown and Frederick Douglass had envisioned years before.

In the West, Grant had proved himself a skilled tactician and, at times, a brilliant strategist. Slowly, with the help of growing numbers of black soldiers, he reversed Union fortunes in the East and the great weight that had begun to settle on Lee's shoulders after Gettysburg soon became a crushing burden.

As the Confederacy disintegrated in Virginia, Sherman headed north, burned Columbia, South Carolina, and crossed into North Carolina, where he was harassed at Bentonville by Confederate General Joseph E. Johnston—who had fought in Virginia and the West and had been chased by Sherman through the South. Johnston was forced to retreat and hearing of Lee's surrender to Grant—near Appomattox Courthouse, in Virginia, on April 9, 1865—halted to await his fate. Sherman, who had burned his way across the South, suddenly became an advocate of charity. The terms he offered Johnston were too liberal to suit Secretary of War Stanton, who had stayed on after Lincoln died, on April 15.

In view of the high degree of bitterness generated by the destruction of the town of Darien by black soldiers and the coming need for all the peoples of America to work together to bring order out of chaos, it is fortunate that Sherman took no black soldiers with him as he waged his ruthless war against the South. About the raid on Darien, Shaw wrote, "Besides my own distaste for this barbarous sort of warfare, I am not sure it will not harm very much the reputation of black troops and those connected with them." Had thousands of black soldiers taken part in Sherman's cruel march through Georgia and the Carolinas, the damage to the reputation of black people and black troops in particular might have been irreparable.

As it was, during the Civil War, a great body of black men began an enduring struggle for respect and for equality. Not long before Lee's surrender, Lincoln told his countrymen that he believed that the many regiments of black soldiers that had fought for the Union had, at last, tipped the balance in its favor.

SELECTED BIBLIOGRAPHY

Robert Gould Shaw lived in a time when his country was in crisis so there are countless books, newspaper articles, manuscript materials—including letters and military documents—and drawings and photographs that illuminate the time in which he lived.

So much has been written about Abraham Lincoln that I have chosen not to list books on Lincoln. From Lincoln's own pen, came a vast and impressive literature. A student would do well to begin with short biographies, move on to longer works—in which Lincoln is quoted liberally—and then study Lincoln's writings. For a time, the most popular biography of Lincoln was Carl Sandburg's three volume work, but so much of it is fanciful that it is unreliable.

In writing this biography, I quoted parts of privately printed volumes of Shaw's letters found at Harvard University's Houghton Library and the rare book and manuscripts division of the New York Public Library. These included childhood letters. It should be noted that most of Shaw's letters covering his participation in the Civil War are now available in a single volume. Since it includes texts of letters I might have missed, this work—edited and with an introduction by Russell Duncan—was invaluable to me.

The list that follows represents a sampling of the material that served as the basis for my text. Some of the books listed here are available in more than one edition.

Aptheker, Herbert, editor. *A Documentary History of the Negro People in the United States.* New York: The Citadel Press, 1969. Edited and with extensive notes by a passionate historian. W. E. B. Du Bois—a prolific scholar and an energetic spokesman for his fellow black Americans—wrote in his preface to the book, "At long last we have this work which rescues from oblivion and loss the very words and thoughts of American Negroes who lived slavery, serfdom and quasi-freedom in the United States of America from the seventeenth to the twentieth century."

Atkinson, Edward, editor. *The Monument to Robert Gould Shaw: Its Inception, Completion and Unveiling 1865–1897.* Boston: Municipal Printing Office, 1897. An important record, published at the time of the unveiling of the Saint-Gaudens monument.

Boyer, Richard O. *The Legend of John Brown.* New York: Alfred A. Knopf, 1973. This is the first volume of an uncompleted work. It contains vivid portraits of distinguished abolitionists.

Brooks, Van Wyck. *The Flowering of New England, 1815–1865.* New York: E.P. Dutton & Co., 1957. A literary history of New England in Shaw's time.

Burchard, Peter. *One Gallant Rush.* New York: St. Martin's Press, 1965. The first biography of Shaw, which became a major historical source for the motion picture *Glory.*

———. *Glory.* New York: St. Martin's Press, Inc., 1990. The 1965 biography listed under a new title.

Catton, Bruce. *The Centennial History of the Civil War,* in three volumes. Garden City: Doubleday & Co., 1961–1965. This and other works by Catton are good military histories, but Catton gave less attention than he should have to the more than 200,000 black Americans who served the Union on both land and sea.

Child, Lydia Maria. *Letters of Lydia Maria Child,* with an introduction by John Greenleaf Whittier. Boston: Houghton Mifflin Co., 1882. The letters of a writer, a devoted abolitionist and close friend of Shaw's mother.

Churchill, Winston S. *The American Civil War.* New York: The Fairfax Press, 1985. Taken from the author's monumental *History of the English Speaking Peoples,* this is a short, accessible account of the political and military conflict.

Cook, Adrian. *The Armies of the Streets: The New York City Draft Riots of 1863.* Lexington: Univeristy of Kentucky Press, 1974.

Cornish, Dudley Taylor. *The Sable Arm.* New York: Longmans Green & Co., 1956. A general history of black participation in the Civil War. Probably the first book of its kind published in the 20th century.

Douglass, Frederick. *The Frederick Douglass Papers,* edited by John W. Blassingame et al. New Haven: Yale University Press, 1979–1992. A collection of Douglass's own extensive writings, in four volumes.

Du Bois, W. E. B. *John Brown.* New York: International Publishers, Co., 1968. An interesting view of Brown by an impassioned and prolific black American scholar.

Emilio, Luis F. *A Brave Black Regiment: History of the Fifty-Fourth Regiment of Massachusetts Volunteer Infantry.* Boston: The Boston Book Co., 1891. A straightforward history, written by an officer who served with the regiment.

Fite, Emerson David. *The Presidential Campaign of 1860.* New York: The Macmillan Co., 1911. A guide to the events of the campaign.

Foner, Philip S. *The Life and Writings of Frederick Douglass.* New York: International Publishers, 1950–1955. An excellent biography by a historian whose works span much of the history of America.

Foote, Shelby. *The Civil War, a Narrative,* in two volumes. New York: Random House, 1958–1974. This history by a gentle Southerner, is essential to an understanding of the Civil War.

Forten, Charlotte L. *The Journals of Charlotte Forten Grimke,* edited and with preface by Brenda Stevenson. New York: Oxford University Press, 1988. Her diaries—1854–92. Stevenson's preface is an important source of information.

Franklin, John Hope. *The Emancipation Proclamation.* Garden City, Doubleday and Co., 1963. A clear, explanatory monograph.

Garrison, William Lloyd. *The Letters of William Lloyd Garrison,* edited by Walter M. Merrill and Louis Ruchames. Cambridge: Belknap Press of Harvard University Press, 1971–1981. His letters in six volumes.

Glatthaar, Joseph T. *Forged in Battle: The Civil War Alliance of Black Soldiers and White Officers.* New York: The Free Press, 1990.

Gooding, James Henry. *On the Altar of Freedom.* Amherst: University of Massachusetts Press, 1991. Letters written by a black soldier of the Fifty Fourth Massachusetts Regiment. These letters seem more the notes of an observer than a participant.

Gordon, George H. *Brook Farm to Cedar Mountain in the War of the Rebellion.* Boston: James R. Osgood & Co., 1883. A memoir by one of Shaw's commanding officers.

Higginson, Henry Lee. *Four Addresses.* Boston: The Merrymount Press, 1902. Includes an address entitled *Robert Gould Shaw.*

Higginson, Thomas Wentworth. *Army Life in a Black Regiment.* East Lansing: Michigan State University Press, 1960. An account, by a leading abolitionist, of his term as colonel of the first Civil War regiment made up of liberated slaves.

Horton, James Oliver and Lois E. *Black Bostonians.* New York and London: Holmes and Meier, 1979. The story of a settlement of black Bostonians.

Kemble, Fanny. *Journal of Residence on a Georgia Plantation in 1838–1839,* edited and with an introduction by John Anthony Scott. New York: Alfred A. Knopf, 1961 and Athens: University of Georgia Press, 1983. Written straight from the heart. A masterpiece. Must be read by anyone who wants to comprehend slave conditions in America.

———. *Further Records 1848–1883.* New York: Henry Holt and Co., 1891. Informative but much less important than her early journal.

Kirstein, Lincoln, with photographs by Richard Benson. *Lay This Laurel: an Album on the Saint-Gaudens Memorial on Boston Common, Honoring Black and White Men Together, who Served the Union Cause with Robert Gould Shaw and Died with Him, July 18, 1963.* New York: Eakins Press, 1973. Kirstein's essays on both Shaw and Saint-Gaudens are short but informative. The photographs—most of them of the memorial when it was in poor condition—by a distinguished graphic artist are magnificent.

Lader, Lawrence. *The Bold Brahmins.* New York: E.P. Dutton & Co., 1961. Contains an excellent short biography of Shaw.

Leng, Charles W. *Staten Island and Its People.* New York: Lewis Historical Publishing Company, 1930. Includes a history of the island in Shaw's time.

McPherson, James M. *Battle Cry of Freedom: The Civil War Era.* New York: Oxford University Press, 1988. A history of the Civil War, in which black Americans are given the importance they deserve.

————. *The Negro's Civil War: How American Negroes Felt and Acted During the War for the Union.* New York: Pantheon Books, 1965. In fashioning this book, the author made liberal use of the words of black soldiers and civilians. As does Aptheker's work, this book helps set the record straight.

Morison, Samuel Eliot. *The Maritime History of Massachusetts, 1783–1860.* Boston: Houghton Mifflin, 1961. By a great sailor and maritime historian, this book is a good source of information on New England's trade with China.

Nevins, Allan. *The Ordeal of the Union.* New York: Scribner's, 1947. A monumental history of the Civil War, in eight volumes, by one of America's great historians.

Oates, Stephen B. *To Purge This Land with Blood.* New York: Harper and Row, 1970. Concentrates on John Brown's later years.

Pearson, Henry Greenleaf. *The Life of John A. Andrew,* in two volumes. Boston and New York: Houghton Mifflin & Co., 1900. An excellent biography.

Preston, Dickson J. *Young Frederick Douglass: The Maryland Years.* Baltimore: Johns Hopkins University Press, 1980. The result of a thorough exploration of the great man's early years.

Quarles, Benjamin. *Frederick Douglass.* New York: The Associated Press Publishers, 1948. An excellent biography by a black American writer.

————. *The Negro in the Civil War.* Boston: Little Brown & Co., 1953. One of several good accounts of roles played by black Americans.

Quint, Alonzo Hall. *Record of the Second Massachusetts Infantry.* Boston: James P. Walker, 1867. A history of the regiment in which Shaw served as a lieutenant and a captain and fought in several battles, notably at Antietam.

Saint-Gaudens, Augustus. *The Reminiscences of Augustus Saint-Gaudens,* edited and amplified by his brother, Homer Saint-Gaudens. New York: The Century Co., 1913. This work, in two volumes, is essential to the study of the life of the sculptor.

Scott, John Anthony and Robert Alan. *John Brown of Harper's Ferry.* New York: Facts On File, Inc-., 1988. A short biography, notable for fresh insights and balanced presentation.

Shaw, Robert Gould. *Letters.* Cambridge: Cambridge University Press, 1864. Mostly letters written while in military service.

———. *Memorial.* Cambridge: Cambridge University Press, 1864. Contains not only Shaw's own words but letters of condolence and excerpts from newspaper accounts of events concerning him.

———. *Letters.* New York: Collins and Brother, 1876. Shaw's letters, written in boyhood and youth.

———. *Blue-Eyed Child of Fortune: The Civil War Letters of Robert Gould Shaw,* edited and with an introduction by Russell Duncan and a preface by William McFeely. Athens: University of Georgia Press, 1992.

Stowe, Harriet Beecher. *Uncle Tom's Cabin: or Life Among the Lowly.* Boston: John P. Jewett and Company, 1852. A fictional account of the tragedy of slavery.

Swinton, William. *History of the Seventh Regiment National Guard, State of New York, During the War of the Rebellion.* New York: Charles T. Dillingham, 1886. A history of the elite regiment in which Shaw began his military life.

Tocqueville, Alexis de. *Journey to America.* New Haven: Yale University Press, 1960. A fascinating and insightful record written by a young Frenchman not long before Shaw's birth.

Wilson, Edmund. *Patriotic Gore: Studies in the Literature of the American Civil War.* New York: Oxford University Press, 1962. Pithy essays on the literature of the war, including comments on the works of Abraham Lincoln, William Tecumseh Sherman, Charlotte Forten and Thomas Wentworth Higginson, all four of whom are mentioned often in this book.

INDEX

Italic page numbers indicate illustrations.

A

abolitionists *See also* slavery;
 names of individuals (e.g.,
 Garrison, William Lloyd)
  Conscription Act riots 6
  Harper's Ferry raid 40–42
  Quakers 53
  women as 16
Adams, Charles Francis 44
Adams, John Quincy 13
Alabama 30
Alexander II, Czar (Russia) 53
Anaconda Plan 36, 45
Anderson, Robert 30–31
Andrew, John A.
  as Brown supporter 61
  early life 60–61
  and 54th Regiment 1–2, 57–68,
    71, 80–82, 96–97, 102–105
  on Hallowell 69
  on Lincoln 25
  and Shaw Memorial 110–114
Antietam, Battle of 6, 44, 49–52, 65
Appleton, John W. M. 62–63, 89
Army of Northern Virginia 46
Army of Virginia 46
Atlanta campaign 116–117
Auld, Hugh 65–66

B

balloons 47
Baltimore, Md. 33
Banks, Nathaniel 35, 37, 45–50
Beaufort, S.C. 76

Beaumont, Gustave de 13
Beauregard, Pierre Gustave
  Toutant 30–31, 36, 92–93,
  100–101, 109
Bell, John 25, 29
Bentonville, N.C. 118
Black Committee 50, 65, 73
Bloody Monday 23
Bonham, Milledge Luke 98
Boston (steamer) 33
Boston, Mass. 12, 24, 72–73, 74,
  114
Boston Courier (newspaper) 14
Boston Pilot (newspaper) 72–73
Brazil 53
Breckenridge, John C. 25, 29
Brook Farm 16–17
Brooks, Preston 29, 54
Brown, John 39–43, 54, 61, 65, 77,
  118
Bull Run
  1st Battle of 36, 54, 93
  2nd Battle of 47–49
Bunker Hill, Battle of ix
Burns, Anthony 28
Burns, Kenneth xi
Burnside, Ambrose 51–52
Butler, Benjamin 45
Butler, Pierce 21, 80, 109
Butler, Sallie 98

C

Camp Meigs 67
Canada 53

125

M

Manassas Junction *See* Bull Run, 1st Battle of
Mansfield, Joseph 50–52
Maryland *38*
McClellan, George E. 35–36, 45–51
McPherson, James M. xi
Meade, George 115
Merrimack (ship) 45
Mexico 27, 53
Milliken's Bend ix
Mississippi 30
Mississippi River 36
Missouri Compromise (1820–21) 26, 28
Mitchell, Nelson 98–99
Monitor (ship) 45
Monroe, Henry A. *94*
Montgomery, James 77, 79–80, 91, 104, 109
Morison, Samuel Eliot 11, 23
Morris Island 1–2, 4, 81, 84, 100
Morse, Charles 52
Murray, Anna 66

N

Netherlands 53
Neuchatel (Switzerland) 19
New Bedford Mercury, The (newspaper) 93
Newbury Herald, The (newspaper) 14
New Madrid, Mo. 46
New Orleans, La. 26, 37, 45
New York City
    Conscription Act riots 6

O

observation balloons *See* balloons
Olustee, Battle of 101–102
One Hundredth New York Regiment 91

P

panic of 1858 24

Parker, Theodore 17, 41
Parkman, Elias 11
Patterson, Robert 35, 37
Paul Jones (gunboat) 79
Pawnee (gunboat) 95
pay disputes 81–82, 102–105
Peninsular Campaign 47–48
Petigrew, James L. 75
Philadelphia, Pa. 67
Phillips, Wendell 70, 73, 114
picket line 84
Pierce, Edward 5–6, 92, 96, 107
Pocotaligo, S.C. 102
Pope, John A. 46–49
Port Hudson ix
Port Royal Experiment 82
Port Royal Island 76
Portugal 53
Potomac River 45
presidential campaign (1860) 25, 29–30
prisoners of war 3, 97–99
Putnam, Haldimand S. 91

Q

Quakers 15, 53
Quint, Alonzo 53

R

Reflector, The (newspaper) 85
Republican Party 29
revolutionary war ix, 11, 14
Rhett, Robert Barnwell 76
rice 12
Richmond, Va.
    Peninsular Campaign 45
riots, draft (New York City) 6
Rogers, Seth 107
Roulet, Monsieur and Madame 19
Russel, Cabot 2, 85, 88–89
Russell, Henry Sturgis 17, 34, *41*, 42, 47
Russia 53

S

St. Helena 3, 81–82
St. Simons Island 77
Saint-Gaudens, Augustus 74,
110–114
Salem Gazette, The (newspaper) 14
Savage, James *41*, 42, 47
Scott, Winfield 35–36
secession 29–30
Second Massachusetts Regiment
Antietam, Battle of 6, 44, 51–52
Shaw service 7, 23, 34
Shenandoah campaign 37
winter quarters (1861) 39
Second South Carolina Infantry ix,
77
Seven Days Battle 45–46
Seventh New York National Guard
See Seventh Regiment
Seventh Regiment 31–33, 110
Seymour, Truman 5, 90, 102
Shaw, Anna (sister) 12–13, 109
Shaw, Coolidge (uncle) 18
Shaw, Ellen ("Nellie") (sister) 13,
46, 73
Shaw, Francis George (father)
11–13, 17, 57–59, 70–71, 106, 108
Shaw, John (ancestor) 11
Shaw, Josephine (sister) 13, 70,
84
Shaw, Robert Gould *20, 32, 41, 60*
abolitionism 16, 37
at Antietam 6, 50–52
on black soldiers 37
Brown influence 42–43
at Bull Run 36
burial of 95, 106
at Cedar Mountain 47
childhood 11–19
death of 10
on discipline 68–69
education 19–24
European travels 19–22
family of 11–19
and 54th Regiment
Andrew meeting 59–60
bravery of 6

command offer 57–59
Darien affair 79–80, 87, 109,
118
departure of 75
Fort Wagner assault 1–10,
87–96
Hilton Head arrival 76
James Island skirmish 84–87
parade review 70–74
pay disputes 81–82
recruitment of 61–68
significance of ix–x
training of 67–70
Forten and 82–84
Hallowell and 2
on Higginson 76–77
leadership skills 5
on Lincoln 33
Lincoln meeting 34
and Lincoln presidential run 25
marriage of 70
memorial to *See* Shaw Memorial
on Montgomery 77
on Pope 46
promotion of 46
on secession 30–31
in Second Massachusetts Regiment 6, 34
in Seventh Regiment 31–33
in Shenandoah campaign 37
Simkins on 63
on *Uncle Tom's Cabin* 21
in Washington defense force 31–
35
in Winchester skirmish 46
Shaw, Samuel (great-great uncle)
11
Shaw, Sarah Blake Sturgis
(mother) 11, 16, 58–59, 69, 106
Shaw, Susanna ("Susie") (sister)
13, 24, 30
Shaw Memorial *74*, 110–114,
112–113
Shenandoah campaign 35, 37, 45
Sherman, William Tecumseh 116,
118